# THE LOST NORWEGIAN

RECIPES FROM SCANDINAVIA AND BEYOND

*by*

CHRISTIN DRAKE

*photography by*

PAULA JANSEN

NORTHLAND PUBLISHING

# CONTENTS

# CONTENTS

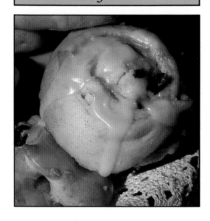

## Dedication

THIS BOOK IS DEDICATED TO MY CHILDREN,
KJERSTI, THOR, AND BJØRN.

## Acknowledgments

SPECIAL THANKS TO MY HUSBAND, STEVE,
MY MOM, RITA FJELD, AND MY FRIENDS
PAM VAN WYCK, DEBBIE LIBER, LINDA
COUDERE, NINA GRØHNVOLD, STEPHANIE
BROWN, ARLEEN MARTINS, AND QINA GILL
WHO HAVE HELPED IN VARIOUS WAYS TO
MAKE THIS COOKBOOK POSSIBLE.

FIRST EDITION

ISBN 0-87358-526-7
Library of Congress Catalog Card Number 91-52601
Cataloging-in-Publication Data
Drake, Christin.
The Lost Norwegian : recipes from Scandinavia
and beyond / by Christin Drake ; photographs
by Paula Jansen. -- 1st ed.
208 p.
Includes index.
ISBN 0-87358-526-7 (hardcover) : $27.50
1. Cookery, Scandinavian. 2. Lost Norwegian
(Restaurant) I. Title.
TX722.A1D73 1991
641.5948--dc20                91-52601 CIP
Designed by Larry Lindahl
Typography by Triad Design, Inc., Prescott
Manufactured in Hong Kong by Dai Nippon

8-91/7.5M/0349

Christin (left) and sister,
Marianne, at 17th of May celebration.

# WHEN I WAS FIVE, I THOUGHT EATING WAS A WASTE OF TIME AND ATE AS LITTLE AS MY MOM WOULD LET ME GET AWAY WITH.

I remember spending an hour picking the onions out of the spaghetti sauce. ♥ I didn't start to appreciate food until I was sixteen years old, and then it was because of Ørnulf, my first love. Ørnulf and I worked together in a delicatessen after school. He truly enjoyed food, so instead of drugs, sex, and rock and roll, it was gourmet food, sex, and Scandinavian folk music (not a bad combination). ♥ Later, as a student in Catholic nursing school, the nuns prepared scrumptious treats for those of us who lived in the residence halls—I guess we were their substitute

1

**SJOKOLADEKREM BOLLER.**

300 g gjær
1½ dl kald melk
1 egg
1 s.s. sukker
300 g mel
100 g smør
hver gang.
stå til heving
Kan bli til wienerbrød og eplestenger.

Rør gjær og melk, pisk
egg, tilsett sukker og mel,
elt deigen fort sammen,
kjevl den straks ut
smør på smørret,
kjevl den ut fire ganger,
stå kaldt mellom.
Stek ved 250° i 10 min.

*The author's recipe for Vanilla Pastries*
*(pp. 138–139) written in Norwegian.*

children. The nuns were delighted when I took an interest in learning how to prepare their favorite recipes. ♥ Having graduated from nursing school a few pounds heavier, and armed with recipes to melt hearts, I went traveling for the next six years, mostly in Italy and Greece. I then took a job in a British private school in Athens, which is a very international city. I made friends from all over the world. Often, we would spend the weekend in the kitchen creating wonderful feasts and learning the tricks of the food trade from one another. Sadly, many recipes were lost due to the amount of wine we consumed while preparing the food, but it was the best of times. ♥ One night, sampling the local cuisine at a Greek tavern, I met my husband-to-be, Steve, an American. After three years

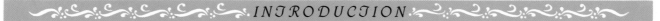

*The Drake family, from left: Kjersti, Steve, Christin, Thor.*

and two children, Kjersti and Thor, Steve talked me into moving from Athens to Flagstaff, Arizona, where we had another child, Bjørn. ♥ Coming to America was a big shock after the carefree life in Europe. Here, the houses aren't very close together and the windows are usually closed. I was used to my Greek neighbors yelling out the window when I got home from work—one would tell me how many times my phone had rung and describe in great detail who had been at my door. Another would yell for me not to make dinner because she was bringing over a tray of moussaka. Another might say she'd helped herself to a piece of my cake when she replaced the milk that she borrowed yesterday, and could she have the recipe. ♥ I also had to change my ways of shopping. In America, it takes only an hour instead of half a day, as in Europe, and you can't become the best of friends with the butcher and the baker. American dairy products don't taste like the real thing to me. I was also disappointed that the restaurants in Flagstaff held few pleasant surprises. ♥ After living here for four years and working as a preschool teacher, I met some people who owned an old Victorian house with a couple of small shops in it. They were looking for somebody to open a restaurant in the building, which didn't sound half bad; after looking into it, I fell in love with the Victorian house and with the idea of having a restaurant. Three months later, it was a reality. I opened The Lost Norwegian Restaurant and worked long hours for the next two years. (I chose the name because, after all, I am Norwegian and have always felt a little bit lost in this new, strange land.) ♥ The recipes in this book represent many stages of my life. Some are traditional Norwegian and come from my mother or aunt. A couple are from my neighbor in Greece, while still others are original recipes from my lifetime of experimenting in the kitchen. All were served at my restaurant. ♥ All but three of the recipes can be

*Simple and relaxing, the atmosphere of The Lost Norwegian Restaurant offered a touch of Norway.*

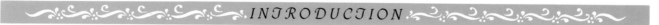

# INTRODUCTION

made using your own kitchen implements. The monks, crumb cake, and farmboy cookies require a monk pan, krumkake iron, and krumkake pinne, which are typical Scandinavian cookware and may be purchased in a specialty kitchen store. ♥ In Norway, we use lots of cheeses like gjetost (goat cheese) and Jarlsburg, all of which may be found in the specialty cheese section of your favorite grocery store; you may substitute your favorite cheeses if you find the flavors too strong or if you just don't feel like making a special trip to the store. You may also substitute Nutrasweet or sugar-free products where appropriate and berries of your choice in all of the recipes calling for them. ♥ The recipes are arranged by months of the year and utilize ingredients appropriate to each month or season—especially fresh fruits and vegetables. Two of our favorite and most important holidays are 17 Mai—our Independence Day—and Christmas. ♥ Enjoy the recipes. I hope you find them tasty and well worth preparing!

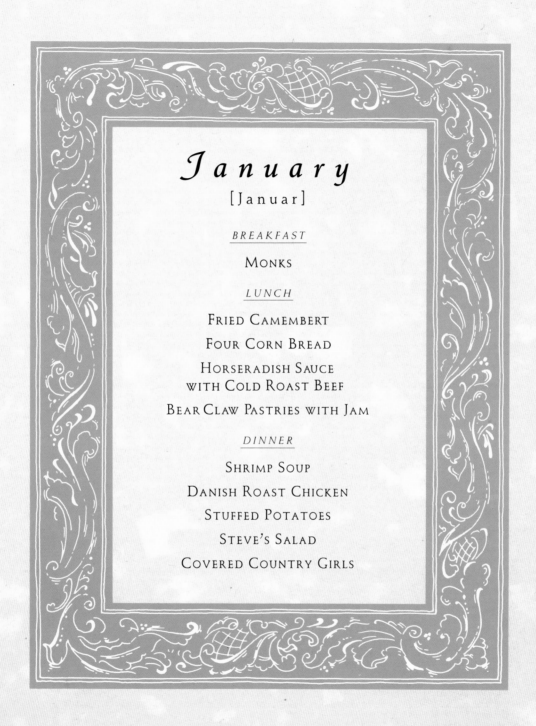

# January

## [Januar]

### *BREAKFAST*

Monks

### *LUNCH*

Fried Camembert

Four Corn Bread

Horseradish Sauce
with Cold Roast Beef

Bear Claw Pastries with Jam

### *DINNER*

Shrimp Soup

Danish Roast Chicken

Stuffed Potatoes

Steve's Salad

Covered Country Girls

# Monks
## [ M o n k e r ]

*Monks are best described as pancake balls.*

In a bowl, beat the butter with the egg yolks, milk, sugar, and salt. Add the flour, baking powder, and cardamom. Stir until there are no lumps. Beat egg whites separately until stiff and fold into the batter.

Heat the monk pan until hot. (If the pan is too hot, the monks will be doughy inside and burned on the outside.) Spoon ½ teaspoon margarine or butter into each cup. Pour 2 tablespoons batter into each cup and turn with a skewer until balls are round and light brown on all sides. Remove and sprinkle with powdered sugar.

– SERVES 4 –

½ CUP BUTTER, MELTED

4 EGGS, SEPARATED

1 CUP MILK

4 TEASPOONS SUGAR

¼ TEASPOON SALT

1 ¾ CUP ALL-PURPOSE FLOUR

2 TEASPOONS BAKING POWDER

½ TEASPOON GROUND CARDAMOM
 OR VANILLA

1 TABLESPOON MARGARINE
 OR BUTTER

½ CUP POWDERED SUGAR

*NOTE: This recipe requires a monk pan, a cast-iron skillet with small round cups in it, common in Scandinavia. You may purchase one at your favorite kitchen specialty store.*

# *Fried Camembert*
[Stekt Ost]

*Camembert is a soft, surface-ripened French cheese available at most grocery stores.*

Divide Camembert into four equal portions and roll each in the flour, then in the egg, and finally in the bread crumbs. Fry in hot oil for 3 minutes and drain on paper towels. Serve hot with a slice of red pepper and parsley.

– SERVES 4 –

8 OUNCES CAMEMBERT

3 TEASPOONS FLOUR

1 EGG

4 TEASPOONS BREAD CRUMBS

OIL FOR FRYING

1 package Yeast

2 cups warm Water

½ cup Yogurt

¼ cup Oil

½ cup Sesame Seeds

½ cup Whole Wheat Flour

½ cup Whole Wheat Rye

½ cup finely ground Rye

6½ cups Wheat Flour

# Four Corn Bread
[Fire Korn Brød]

Stir yeast in warm water. Add yogurt and oil. Fold in the sesame seeds and add all remaining ingredients except ½ cup of the wheat flour. Knead until smooth. Cover the dough with a tea towel and set aside to rise for 45 minutes. Punch the dough down and knead a bit using the rest of the flour. Form into a loaf. Let rise until doubled in size (approximately 45 minutes). Bake at 350° for about 40 minutes.

– Makes 1 Loaf –

WHEAT

RYE

## Horseradish Sauce with Cold Roast Beef
### [Kald Biff med Pepperrot]

Combine sauce ingredients and spread 1 tablespoon on each roast beef slice. Roll slices and garnish with parsley and red paprika. Serve cold.

– SERVES 4 –

4 TABLESPOONS MAYONNAISE

1 TEASPOON STONE GROUND MUSTARD

2 TABLESPOONS SOUR CREAM

1 TEASPOON HORSERADISH, PUREED

¼ TEASPOON PEPPER

1 POUND ROAST BEEF, COOKED, COLD, SLICED

*A portrait of the author's parents on their wedding day accents a setting of Horseradish Sauce with Cold Roast Beef and Fried Camembert.*

# Bear Claw Pastries with Jam

[Bjørne Lab Winerbrød med Syltetøy]

In a bowl, mix water, yeast, and sugar. Set aside for 5 minutes.

In large bowl, pour 4 cups flour. Add yeast mixture, milk, eggs, salt, cardamom, and vanilla. Mix with hands, then knead for 10 minutes. Cool dough in refrigerator for 30 minutes.

Using some of the remaining flour, roll pastry to ¼″ thickness. Cover ⅓ of the pastry dough with ⅓ of the butter. Fold the unbuttered portion of the pastry over the buttered portion. Refrigerate for 15 minutes. Roll, butter, and fold dough again using the same procedure as above. Refrigerate for 15 minutes. Repeat the process once more using the last of the butter.

½ CUP WARM WATER

2 PACKAGES YEAST

½ CUP SUGAR

5½ CUPS FLOUR

½ CUP COLD MILK

2 EGGS, BEATEN

1 TEASPOON SALT

¼ TEASPOON GROUND CARDAMOM

1 TEASPOON VANILLA

1 POUND COLD, UNSALTED BUTTER

1 16-OUNCE JAR JAM

ICING

1 CUP POWDERED SUGAR

1 TEASPOON LEMON JUICE

2 TABLESPOONS WATER

Roll dough to ¼″ thick. Cut into rectangles 5″ long by 2½″ wide. Place 1 tablespoonful of jam along top part of rectangle. Place another rectangle on top and seal edges by brushing with water and pressing together. With a knife, make four cuts halfway into dough and bend pastries into crescent shapes until they resemble claws. Cover with a damp tea towel and let rise on greased cookie sheet in warm place for 2 hours. Bake at 350° for about 20 minutes or until golden brown.

ICING

Stir all ingredients together. If the icing is not thin enough (it should be runny), add a few more drops of water. Drizzle icing over the pastries when they have cooled.

– MAKES 24 PASTRIES –

# Shrimp Soup
[Reke Suppe]

Bring water and salt to a boil. Add shrimp, cover, and simmer until red. Remove shrimp and peel. Set aside.

Bring chicken stock and sage to a boil. Add the shrimp water, being careful not to include the cloudy material that has settled on the bottom of the pan.

In skillet, sauté mushrooms briefly in a little oil and add mushrooms to the mixture. Add remaining vegetables. Let the soup simmer until vegetables are soft. Add shrimp, sherry, and parsley just before serving. Serve hot.

– SERVES 4 TO 6 –

2½ CUPS WATER

½ TEASPOON SALT

½ POUND SHRIMP

2 CUPS CHICKEN STOCK

½ TEASPOON SAGE

½ CUP MUSHROOMS, SLICED

2 TABLESPOONS OIL

1 CUP ASPARAGUS, CUT INTO SMALL BITS

½ CUP YELLOW ZUCCHINI, SLICED

6 GREEN ONIONS, CHOPPED

½ CUP GREEN PEAS

2 TABLESPOONS SHERRY

2 TABLESPOONS CHOPPED PARSLEY

# *Danish Roast Chicken*
## [Dansk Høne]

Preheat oven to 375°. Rub the chicken with oil and sprinkle with paprika, salt, and pepper. Arrange chicken on a roasting pan. Stuff the parsley inside the cavity with the butter. Reduce oven temperature to 350° and roast chicken for 1 hour and 30 minutes, basting every 20 minutes. Cut into four parts and serve hot.

– SERVES 4 –

1 PLUMP CHICKEN

3 TABLESPOONS OIL

1 TABLESPOON GROUND
   RED PAPRIKA

1 TEASPOON SALT

½ TEASPOON GROUND PEPPER

1 BUNCH PARSLEY

1 TABLESPOON BUTTER

En fjær i kan bli til fem høns.

*One feather can become five hens.*

# Stuffed Potatoes
[Fylte Poteter]

*In Norway, we eat potatoes with just about everything. This recipe is a great alternative to boiled or baked potatoes.*

Preheat oven to 400°. Clean potatoes and rub with salt. Cut a cross on top of each potato and tightly wrap each one in foil. Bake for one hour.

Unwrap the potatoes and cut a "lid" off each one lengthwise. Scoop out the inside, leaving a ½" shell. In a bowl, mash the insides with butter, salt, and pepper. Fill each potato shell with this mixture and sprinkle with grated cheese. Return potatoes to oven and bake for an additional 10 minutes. Serve hot.

– SERVES 4 –

8 MEDIUM POTATOES

2 TABLESPOONS CHOPPED CHIVES

½ CUP BUTTER

1 CUP GRATED CHEDDAR CHEESE

SALT AND PEPPER TO TASTE

# Steve's Salad

[ S t e v e ' s   S a l a t ]

1 bunch Spinach

4 Lettuce leaves

2 ripe Tomatoes

12 Mushrooms

½ Cucumber

½ Red Onion

DRESSING

¼ cup Mayonnaise

¼ cup Heavy Cream or
   Sour Cream

2 teaspoons coarsely
   ground Pepper

¼ teaspoon Tabasco Sauce

Rinse spinach and lettuce well and tear into bits. Cut tomatoes and mushrooms to desired sizes; slice cucumber and onion. Combine in a large bowl.

DRESSING
Combine dressing ingredients in a small bowl or jar and mix well. Arrange salad on individual plates and put 2 tablespoons of dressing on each.

– Serves 4 –

## Covered Country Girls
[Tilsløorte Bondepiker]

Preheat oven to 375°. Peel and cut apples into small pieces. Cook for 20 minutes in a pot with enough water to cover apples. Drain.

Lightly grease the bottom of a shallow baking dish. Layer the bottom of the pan with apples. Beat butter and sugar together until light and foamy. Add egg yolks and vanilla. Beat egg whites separately until stiff and fold gently into the batter. Pour the batter over apples. Sprinkle chopped almonds on top. Bake until golden brown, approximately 30 minutes. Serve warm with whipped cream.

– SERVES 6 –

10 APPLES

WATER TO COVER APPLES

½ POUND BUTTER

1½ CUPS SUGAR

4 EGGS, SEPARATED

1 TEASPOON VANILLA

1½ CUPS CHOPPED ALMONDS

1 PINT HEAVY CREAM, WHIPPED STIFF

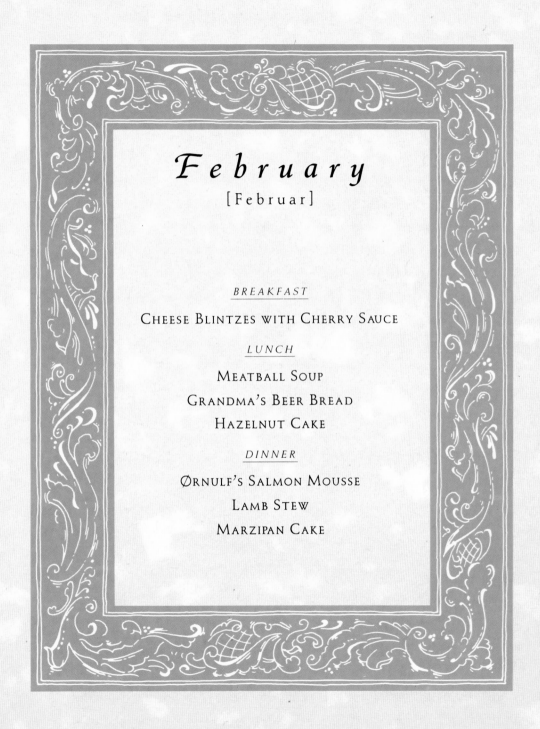

# February

[Februar]

*BREAKFAST*

Cheese Blintzes with Cherry Sauce

*LUNCH*

Meatball Soup

Grandma's Beer Bread

Hazelnut Cake

*DINNER*

Ørnulf's Salmon Mousse

Lamb Stew

Marzipan Cake

# Cheese Blintzes with Cherry Sauce

## [Oste Kaker med Kirse Bær Saus]

*Blintzes are a breakfast treat. Prepare them a day ahead of time and just pop them into the oven in the morning. They will be ready to eat by the time the coffee is made!*

*NOTE: Prepare cherry sauce first so it is ready to eat with the warm blintzes.*

Beat until smooth all ingredients except milk. Add the milk gradually until the batter is even. Melt a small amount of margarine in a frying pan. Pour in a little batter. Fry the pancakes on one side only until the batter is set. Keep pancakes on a warm plate until all are made.

6 Eggs

½ teaspoon Salt

4 tablespoons Oil

1½ cups Flour

4 tablespoons Butter

1¾ cups Milk

1 tablespoon Margarine
    for frying

FILLING

2 CUPS COTTAGE CHEESE

1 EGG

2 TABLESPOONS SUGAR

1 TABLESPOON LEMON JUICE

CHERRY SAUCE

1½ TABLESPOONS CORN STARCH

½ CUP WATER

2 CUPS FRESH OR FROZEN PITTED
CHERRIES

¼ CUP SUGAR

## FILLING

Stir all ingredients together until well blended. Put 2 tablespoons of filling in the middle of each pancake and fold the pancake into a package around the filling. Put the blintzes seam-side down on an oven-proof tray. When you have filled all the blintzes, pour a little melted butter over them. Before serving, heat them in the oven for 10 minutes at 350° or warm them in a frying pan. Makes 12 blintzes.

## CHERRY SAUCE

Stir the corn starch into the water. Add cherries and sugar. Boil for 10 minutes. Serve hot or cold.

– SERVES 4 –

# Meatball Soup
## [Kjøtt Bolle Suppe]

To make the beef broth, I use meat bones and cook them for two hours or more in water. You may also use ready-made beef broth but do not add salt. When broth is ready, place 1½ cups in separate pot for cooking the meatballs. Add spices to the remaining broth. Clean, peel, and chop the vegetables and add them to the broth. Turn the heat down to a simmer and cook for 10 minutes.

Mix together all the ingredients for meatballs. Roll into small, marble-sized balls. Bring the 1½ cups of beef broth to a boil and add the meatballs. Cook for 3 minutes, then remove with a slotted spoon. Discard broth.

Add cooked meatballs to soup and let simmer for about 10 minutes, or until vegetables are soft.

– SERVES 6 –

10 cups BEEF BROTH

1 clove GARLIC, CRUSHED

1 pinch ROSEMARY

½ teaspoon THYME

1 pinch OREGANO

6 sprigs GREEN ONION OR
   ½ YELLOW ONION

4 CARROTS

3 POTATOES

3 CELERY STALKS

3 ZUCCHINI, GREEN OR YELLOW

MEATBALLS

¼ pound GROUND BEEF

3 tablespoons FLOUR

1 EGG

⅓ teaspoon SALT

¼ teaspoon PEPPER

½ teaspoon THYME

1½ cups BEEF BROTH

1 package Yeast

1½ cups Milk

4 cups Rye Flour

4 cups Wheat Flour

1 teaspoon Anise

1 teaspoon Coriander

1 teaspoon Pepper

½ tablespoon Sugar

1 cup Raisins

½ cup Dark Molasses

1 bottle Beer

# Grandma's Beer Bread
## [Bestemors Ølle Bød]

*This bread is an old tradition and a meal in itself.*

Dissolve the yeast in ¼ cup of warmed milk.

In a large bowl, combine rye flour, wheat flour, anise, coriander, pepper, sugar, and raisins. Stir until mixed.

In a separate bowl, mix the yeast mixture with the molasses and beer. Add the rest of the milk. Combine this mixture with the flour mixture and knead all ingredients together until dough is smooth but sticky. Put the dough into a bowl, cover with a tea towel, and set aside in a warm place for 2 hours.

Punch the bread down and knead for 10 minutes using more flour if necessary. Form into two loaves and set aside in a floured pan to rise for 4 hours or overnight. Bake at 350° for 30 to 40 minutes.

– MAKES 2 LOAVES –

# Hazelnut Cake
[Haselnøtt Kake]

*Haselnøtt kake tastes best the day after baking.*

Preheat oven to 350°. Grease and flour a 9″ spring pan (regular cake pan will do). Beat butter and sugar until light and fluffy. Mix in flour, baking powder, and salt. Add milk and vanilla. In separate bowl, beat egg whites until stiff and fold into batter.

Pour half of the batter into cake pan. Sprinkle with chocolate and nuts. Pour remaining batter over chocolate and nuts. Bake at 350° for 30 minutes or until fork comes out clean.

## FROSTING

Melt the butter and chocolate in a pot over low heat. Add water and vanilla and stir until smooth. Take the pot off the heat and beat in egg yolks. Pour the hot frosting over the cake. Sprinkle chopped hazelnuts over top.

¼ POUND BUTTER

1 CUP SUGAR

2 CUPS FLOUR

2 TEASPOONS BAKING POWDER

½ TEASPOON SALT

1 CUP MILK

1 TEASPOON VANILLA

4 EGG WHITES

½ CUP GRATED SWEET CHOCOLATE

1 CUP CHOPPED HAZELNUTS

FROSTING

1 TABLESPOON BUTTER

4 SQUARES SWEET CHOCOLATE

3 TABLESPOONS WATER

1 TEASPOON VANILLA

2 EGG YOLKS

4 TABLESPOONS CHOPPED HAZELNUTS

# Ørnulf's Salmon Mousse
## [Ørnulf's Faesert Laks]

*This is a dish that sounds fancy but is very simple to make.*
*Prepare double portions and serve as a main course.*

Preheat oven to 350°. Cut the salmon into four portions and arrange in a baking dish. Combine deboned orange roughy, egg, cream, parsley, tarragon, lemon juice, salt, and pepper in a blender. Blend into a thick paste. Put into a pastry tube with a wide tip. Sprinkle a little salt on the salmon and top with equal portions of the fish paste. Pour wine into the dish and bake at 350° for 15 minutes. Serve warm garnished with lemon slices and lettuce.

– SERVES 4 –

1 POUND SALMON

½ POUND ORANGE ROUGHY,
    DEBONED

1 EGG

¼ CUP CREAM

1 TABLESPOON PARSLEY, CHOPPED

½ TEASPOON TARRAGON

1 TEASPOON LEMON JUICE

SALT AND PEPPER TO TASTE

½ CUP WHITE WINE

1 LEMON, SLICED

LETTUCE FOR GARNISH

3 POUNDS LAMB, VEAL, OR
   TENDER BEEF

4 TABLESPOONS OIL

6 CUPS WATER

1 CUP RED WINE

4 TABLESPOONS TOMATO PASTE

½ TEASPOON CINNAMON

¼ TEASPOON PEPPER

½ TEASPOON SALT

½ TEASPOON ROSEMARY

¼ TEASPOON OREGANO

2 TEASPOONS MINT

8 SPRIGS GREEN ONIONS

4 POTATOES, CUT UP

6 ZUCCHINI, CUT UP

½ POUND FETA CHEESE

# *Lamb Stew*
## [L a m m e   G r y t e]

*This recipe was given to me by a shepherd who used goat meat, which tastes wonderful but is not easy to find. Lamb, veal, and beef are tasty alternatives. Serve this aromatic dish with rice.*

In a skillet, brown the meat in oil. When browned, place the meat into a heavy pot and add the water, wine, tomato paste, and spices. Simmer the stew for 2½ hours. When meat is tender, add chopped vegetables and cook until tender (about 20 minutes longer). Pour the stew into a baking dish. Add more liquid if necessary. Sprinkle feta chunks over the top and place in a 400°-oven or broiler long enough to brown the cheese, about 5 minutes.

– SERVES 4 –

# Marzipan Cake
[Marsipan Kake]

*This cake is often made for special occasions such as birthdays or weddings.*

Preheat oven to 350°. Beat butter and sugar until light and fluffy. Add egg yolks. Sift in the flour, corn starch, and baking powder. Beat egg whites separately until stiff and fold them into the cake batter. Pour the batter into two 9″ greased and floured spring or cake pans. Bake for 30 minutes or until cake comes away from sides of the pans. Let the cakes cool before you take them out of the forms.

WALNUT FILLING

Grind the walnuts in a food processor with egg white and sugar. Beat whipping cream separately until stiff and add to the walnut mixture carefully. Spoon mixture onto one of the cakes and place the other cake on top.

½ CUP BUTTER

1 CUP SUGAR

4 EGGS, SEPARATED

1 CUP FLOUR

1 CUP CORN STARCH

1 TEASPOON BAKING POWDER

WALNUT FILLING

1 CUP GROUND WALNUTS

1 EGG WHITE

1 CUP POWDERED SUGAR

1 CUP HEAVY CREAM

*NOTE: You may substitute pineapple chunks, one 28-ounce can, drained, for the walnut filling.*

MARZIPAN LID AND FLOWERS

2½ CUPS BLANCHED ALMONDS

2 CUPS POWDERED SUGAR

1 EGG WHITE

4 DROPS ALMOND EXTRACT

## MARZIPAN LID AND FLOWERS

Grind the blanched almonds to a very fine flour. Add powdered sugar, egg white, and almond extract. Knead mixture into a dough using powdered sugar as flour.

Roll the marzipan into a thin dough using a rolling pin and powdered sugar as needed. (If you work this dough too hard it will be oily and sticky. Put it in the refrigerator for a while if this is a problem.) Use the cake pan as a pattern. Make a lid and a side out of three-quarters of the dough. Then knead a little food coloring into the remaining dough and create flowers, leaves, animals, or shapes of your choosing.

Lift the marzipan lid carefully onto the cake. Wrap the side around the cake, sealing the seams with a little egg white or water. Arrange flowers or other decorations on top.

*NOTE: You may buy marzipan ready-made in a store; you'll need two rolls.*

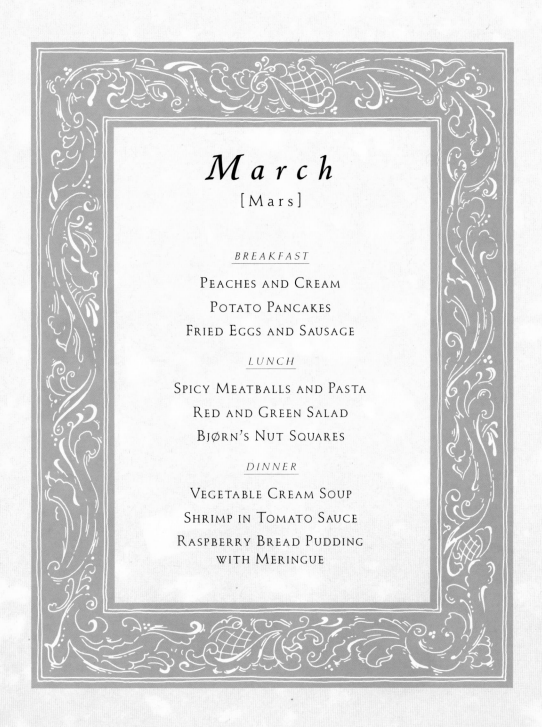

# March

## [Mars]

### BREAKFAST

Peaches and Cream
Potato Pancakes
Fried Eggs and Sausage

### LUNCH

Spicy Meatballs and Pasta
Red and Green Salad
Bjørn's Nut Squares

### DINNER

Vegetable Cream Soup
Shrimp in Tomato Sauce
Raspberry Bread Pudding
with Meringue

# Peaches and Cream
[Ferskner og Krem]

Whip the cream and powdered sugar until stiff. In a tall glass, layer the peaches with the cream ending with a topping of cream. Sprinkle with nutmeg.

– SERVES 4 –

1 PINT HEAVY CREAM

1 TABLESPOON POWDERED SUGAR

1 16-OUNCE CAN PEACHES

$\frac{1}{8}$ TEASPOON NUTMEG

# Potato Pancakes
## [Potet Pannekaker]

4 medium Potatoes

1½ tablespoons grated Onions

2 Eggs, beaten

2 tablespoons Flour

1 teaspoon Salt

½ teaspoon Baking Powder

1 tablespoon Oil for frying

Grate the potatoes. Combine with grated onions, eggs, flour, salt, and baking powder. Mix well. In a hot frying pan, warm the oil and drop 2 tablespoons of the mixture per pancake. Fry until light brown on both sides, turning once. Serve hot.

– Serves 4 –

# Fried Eggs and Sausage
[Stekt Egg med Pølse]

Fry the sausage until done. Set aside in a hot dish to keep warm.

In a moderately hot, clean frying pan, melt the butter. Break one egg at a time close to the pan to prevent it from spreading. When cooked, egg white should be set on top but not brown on the bottom. Serve with the sausage.

– SERVES 4 –

1 POUND BREAKFAST SAUSAGE

2 TABLESPOONS BUTTER
    FOR FRYING

8 EGGS

# Spicy Meatballs and Pasta
[Kjøtboller i Tomat Saus
med Makaroni]

*Double this meatball recipe and freeze half to make for an easy meal another time. The pasta recipe can be a meal in itself: add crushed walnuts and serve with a green salad.*

Mix all ingredients and knead. Form into small, oblong balls. Warm oil in skillet and brown the meatballs on all sides. Set aside. Use the oil left after browning the meatballs to brown the onions for the sauce.

## SAUCE

Chop onions and brown in the skillet. Remove and combine with water, wine, tomato paste, tomato sauce, tomatoes, and spices in a pot. Simmer mixture for 20 minutes. Add meatballs and simmer for another 45 minutes over low heat.

1½ POUNDS GROUND BEEF

1 EGG

4 SLICES BREAD, CUBED

¼ TEASPOON PEPPER

½ TEASPOON OREGANO

½ TEASPOON THYME

1 TABLESPOON OIL FOR FRYING

SAUCE

2 SMALL YELLOW ONIONS

2 CUPS WATER

1 CUP RED WINE

1 6-OUNCE CAN TOMATO PASTE

1 8-OUNCE CAN TOMATO SAUCE

3 SOFT TOMATOES, CHOPPED

(continued on next page)

½ teaspoon Rosemary

1 Bay Leaf

¼ teaspoon Cinnamon

½ teaspoon Basil

½ clove Garlic, crushed

½ cup crushed Walnuts

PASTA

4 tablespoons melted Butter
    or Olive Oil

½ cup Parmesan Cheese, grated

¼ cup Cream

1 Egg Yolk

½ teaspoon Pepper

2 teaspoons Basil

1 pound Rigatoni or other
    kind of pasta

## PASTA

Pour melted butter or oil into a small bowl and add Parmesan, cream, egg yolk, pepper, and basil.

Cook the rigatoni according to package instructions. Drain well and combine with butter and cream mixture. Top with meatball sauce and serve immediately.

– Serves 6 –

# Red and Green Salad

[Rød og Grønn Salat]

Drain peas and dice peppers. Grate or shred cabbage, slice celery and radishes, and chop parsley. Combine in a large bowl and mix well. Line serving bowl with endive leaves and arrange salad in the middle.

DRESSING

Combine dressing ingredients in a bowl or jar and mix well. Pour dressing over the salad and chill for 10 minutes before serving.

– Serves 6 –

2 cups cooked Peas

1 Green Pepper

1 Red Pepper

1 cup Red Cabbage

1 Celery stalk

1 tablespoon Parsley

5 Radishes

1 head of Belgian Endive

DRESSING

3 tablespoons Raspberry
   Vinegar

4 tablespoons Olive Oil

Freshly ground Pepper
   to taste

Salt to taste

Dash of Tabasco or Gin

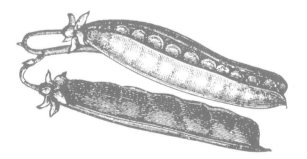

# Bjørn's Nut Squares
[Bjørn's Nøtte Snipper]

¾ CUP SOFTENED BUTTER

2 CUPS SUGAR

4 EGGS

4 TEASPOONS VANILLA

1¾ CUPS FLOUR

1 TEASPOON BAKING POWDER

4 TABLESPOONS COCOA

2 CUPS CRUSHED WALNUTS

1 CUP GROUND ALMONDS

*These nut cookies taste best after a few days and are great for kids' lunches.*

Preheat oven to 350°. Beat butter and sugar. Add eggs, vanilla, flour, baking powder, cocoa, walnuts, and almonds. Beat until well blended. Pour batter into a greased and floured deep-dish baking pan. Bake at 350° for 20 minutes. Cut into squares when cool.

– MAKES 24 SQUARES –

# Vegetable Cream Soup
[Grønnsak Suppe]

*When your vegetable box is full of left-over vegetables, it's time to make this nutritious soup. I like freshly ground pepper on top and a squeeze of lemon juice. A spoon of sour cream on top also adds richness to the soup.*

Cook the vegetables in slightly salted water until soft or use leftover, already cooked vegetables. Put vegetables in a blender or food processor and blend well. Pour into soup pot and add cream and spices. Serve hot or cold.

– SERVES 4 –

6 CUPS CHOPPED VEGETABLES, INCLUDING SPINACH, BROCCOLI, ONIONS, CARROTS, POTATOES, ASPARAGUS, ZUCCHINI

¼ CUP CREAM

½ TEASPOON THYME

1 TEASPOON SALT

½ TEASPOON PEPPER

1 CLOVE GARLIC, CRUSHED

## Shrimp in Tomato Sauce
[ R e k e r   i   T o m a t   S a u s ]

1 cup Water

1 cup White Wine

2 16-ounce cans Tomato Sauce

4 tablespoons Tomato Paste

¼ teaspoon Pepper

1 teaspoon crushed Garlic

½ teaspoon Oregano

1 Bay Leaf

1 Green Pepper, diced

1 cup Snow Peas

1 cup Green Beans

1½ pounds peeled Shrimp

In a skillet or pot, combine water, wine, tomato sauce, tomato paste, and spices. Add vegetables and simmer for 30 minutes. Add shrimp and simmer for another 15 minutes.

– Serves 4 –

# Raspberry Bread Pudding with Meringue
## [Bringebær Brød Pudding med Marengs]

Preheat oven to 350°. Trim crust off bread and cut into cubes. Place in large mixing bowl and set aside.

In another large bowl, combine the milk, egg yolks, sugar, vanilla, nutmeg, lemon juice, grated lemon rind, raisins, and almonds. Beat well and pour over the bread cubes. Stir.

Beat egg whites separately until stiff and fold into the bread mixture. Add the raspberries. Fold carefully until well blended. Pour the bread pudding into a greased oven-proof dish. Set the dish in a water bath (a shallow pan filled with water) and bake for 45 minutes.

5 CUPS BREAD CUBES

3 CUPS MILK

3 EGGS, SEPARATED

½ CUP SUGAR

1½ TEASPOONS VANILLA

¼ TEASPOON NUTMEG

2 TABLESPOONS LEMON JUICE

½ TABLESPOON GRATED LEMON RIND

¼ CUP RAISINS

½ CUP ALMONDS, GROUND

1 CUP RASPBERRIES

MERINGUE

2 Egg Whites

¼ teaspoon Cream of Tartar

4 tablespoons Powdered Sugar

½ teaspoon Vanilla

*NOTE: As an alternative, serve warm with whipped cream or vanilla, cherry, or strawberry sauce instead of meringue.*

## MERINGUE

Beat egg whites with cream of tartar until stiff. Sprinkle in powdered sugar while beating. Add vanilla and continue beating. Pour meringue over bread pudding and bake for another 15 minutes.

– Serves 6 –

*The author's father (seated) and Aunt Ingeborg at her aunt's home in Norway.*

# April
[April]

### BREAKFAST

Orange–Chocolate Chip Muffins

Scrambled Eggs and Ham

### LUNCH

Norwegian Hamburgers

Dark Bread

Danish Pastries

### DINNER

Filled Tomatoes

Chicken in Wine Sauce

Spring Salad

Grandma's Best Ice Cream

# Orange–Chocolate Chip Muffins

[Appelsin og Sjokolade Frokost Brød]

Preheat oven to 375°. Grate the two oranges. Beat the butter with the sugar until soft and add the eggs. Add orange juice and sour cream and beat until smooth. Add remaining ingredients and beat until well blended. Fill prepared muffin tins with batter. Reduce oven temperature to 350° and bake for 20 to 25 minutes.

– Makes 12 Muffins –

2 large Oranges

¾ cup Sugar

½ cup Butter

2 Eggs

½ cup freshly squeezed Orange Juice

½ cup Sour Cream or Yogurt

1¾ cups Flour

¼ cup Wheat Germ

1 teaspoon Baking Powder

½ teaspoon Baking Soda

½ cup small semi-sweet Chocolate Chips

## Scrambled Eggs and Ham
### [Eggerøre og Sinke]

8 Eggs

4 tablespoons Milk

Salt and Pepper to taste

4 tablespoons Margarine
for frying

8 slices fully cooked Ham

In large bowl, beat eggs and milk until well blended. Add salt and pepper. Melt 2 tablespoons margarine over low heat in a non-stick skillet or saucepan. Pour eggs into pan and constantly stir and fold until slightly moist and fluffy. Keep warm between two plates.

Melt 2 tablespoons margarine in skillet or frying pan over medium heat. Arrange ham in pan and fry on both sides until warmed through—approximately 4 minutes. Serve hot.

– Serves 4 –

Jo flere kokker, jo mere søl.
*More cooks, more mess.*

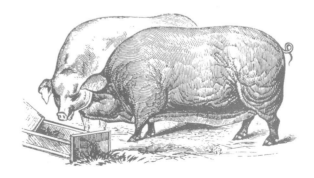

# *Norwegian Hamburgers*
## [Medistekaker]

In a large bowl, combine and knead first seven ingredients. Form into hamburger patties. Fry onion slices in oil or margarine until light brown. Remove from pan. Add patties to frying pan and brown on both sides. Poke the hamburgers with a skewer to make sure they are cooked through. After hamburgers are cooked, add fried onions and warm before serving. Serve with crisp lettuce and some slices of tomato, dark bread and butter, and maybe some blue cheese.

– SERVES 4 –

½ POUND GROUND BEEF

½ POUND GROUND PORK

½ CUP BOILED POTATOES, MASHED

2 TABLESPOONS ONIONS, FINELY CHOPPED

½ TEASPOON PEPPER

½ TEASPOON SALT

1 EGG

2 ONIONS, CUT INTO SLICES

2 TABLESPOONS OIL OR MARGARINE FOR FRYING

1 PLUMP CHICKEN

½ TEASPOON SALT

½ TEASPOON PEPPER

½ BOTTLE WHITE WINE

1 CUP WATER

2 TEASPOONS CHICKEN BOUILLON

2 CLOVES OF GARLIC, CUT IN HALF

½ POUND FRESH MUSHROOMS

1 CUP PITTED GREEN OLIVES

3 TEASPOONS OIL OR MARGARINE
   FOR FRYING

2 TEASPOONS LEMON JUICE

# Chicken in Wine Sauce
[ K y l l i n g   i   W i n   S a u s ]

*If you don't serve an appetizer, double the recipe because everyone will want seconds.*

Divide chicken into four parts and rub with salt and pepper. Brown chicken parts on both sides in a frying pan. Put chicken in a pot and pour wine over it. Add 1 cup of water to the frying pan in which you fried the chicken and boil for five minutes. Add this to chicken. Add more water if necessary to cover the chicken. Add bouillon and garlic and let chicken boil slowly for 40 minutes. While chicken is boiling, sauté whole mushrooms in oil or margarine and set aside. Add mushrooms, olives, and 2 teaspoons lemon juice to the chicken 10 minutes before serving. Salt and pepper to taste. Serve with rice.

– SERVES 4 –

# Spring Salad
[Vår Salat]

Chop apples, tomatoes, celery, and pepper into bite-sized pieces. Tear lettuce and combine with chopped fruit and vegetables in large salad/mixing bowl. Sprinkle with chives.

DRESSING

Mix all dressing ingredients in small bowl or jar. Pour over salad and serve immediately.

– SERVES 4 –

2 APPLES

2 TOMATOES

1 CUP CHOPPED CELERY

1 GREEN PEPPER

6 LETTUCE LEAVES

4 CHIVES

DRESSING

JUICE OF ½ LEMON

¼ CUP WALNUT OR OLIVE OIL

¼ TEASPOON PEPPER

¼ TEASPOON SALT

½ TEASPOON BASIL

1½ cups Powdered Sugar

4 Egg Yolks

1½ cups Heavy Cream

1½ cups fresh Strawberries,
    mashed

8 ounces Sweet Chocolate,
    chopped into small pieces

2 cups fresh Strawberries,
    whole

*NOTE: You may substitute blueberries, rasp-
berries, blackberries, cherries, peaches, or other
fruit for the strawberries.*

# Grandma's Best Ice Cream
[Bestemors Beste Is]

Beat sugar and egg yolks for 10 minutes with electric beater. In a separate bowl, beat cream until stiff and fold into sugar and egg mixture. Add mashed strawberries (if using frozen, be sure to defrost and drain) and chocolate. Blend well. Pour mixture into a round form with a hole in the middle (bundt cake pan or jello mold). Cover with foil and place in freezer for 24 hours.

Remove from freezer 30 minutes before serving. Turn form upside down on a platter and remove. Fill the middle with the whole strawberries and serve.

– Serves 6 –

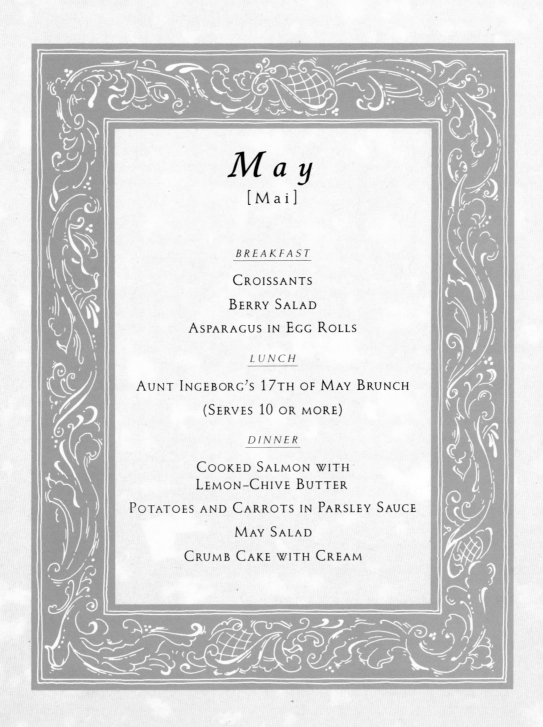

# May
## [Mai]

*BREAKFAST*

CROISSANTS

BERRY SALAD

ASPARAGUS IN EGG ROLLS

*LUNCH*

AUNT INGEBORG'S 17TH OF MAY BRUNCH

(SERVES 10 OR MORE)

*DINNER*

COOKED SALMON WITH
LEMON-CHIVE BUTTER

POTATOES AND CARROTS IN PARSLEY SAUCE

MAY SALAD

CRUMB CAKE WITH CREAM

# Croissants

[Horn]

Preheat oven to 350°. Warm milk in a pot over low heat. Remove ½ cup of warmed milk and add yeast to it. Add sugar to remaining warmed milk. When yeast has dissolved, add flour and sugar-milk mixture. Knead dough on lightly floured surface until smooth and elastic. Refrigerate for 20 minutes.

Roll dough out on a lightly floured surface. Spread one-third of the butter on two-thirds of the dough and fold four times, beginning with the unbuttered portion of the dough. Chill for 15 minutes. Roll, butter, and fold the dough in this way two more times. Roll the dough out a fourth time to 1″ thick. Cut the dough into 5″ squares. Cut each square in half diagonally to make two triangles. Roll triangles and curve into crescent shapes. Place on a baking sheet,

(continued on next page)

1 cup Milk

1½ tablespoons Sugar

1 package Yeast

1½ cups Flour

1¼ cups Butter

1 cup Strawberries

1 cup Blueberries

1 cup Cherries

1 cup Raspberries

¼ cup Water

4 tablespoons Sugar

cover with a towel, and let rise until puffy and doubled in size (about 1½ hours). Bake at 400° for 10 to 15 minutes or until golden brown.

– Makes 12 Croissants –

# Berry Salad
[Bær Salat]

*This salad is the most refreshing of all breakfasts—I could live on this alone.*

Clean berries and cut largest ones in half. Pit cherries and mix with the berries. In a separate bowl, combine sugar and water; stir. Pour sugar water over berries and serve in individual bowls.

– Serves 4 –

1 cup Green Peas

2 cups shredded
    Iceberg Lettuce

1 pound cooked, peeled Shrimp

¼ cup Sour Cream

¼ cup Mayonnaise

2 tablespoons Gin (optional)

½ teaspoon Tabasco Sauce

2 tablespoons Tomato Catsup

Juice of ½ Lemon

½ teaspoon White Pepper

1 teaspoon Dill

1 Lemon, sliced

# Shrimp Salad
[Reke Salat]

*In Oslo, where I grew up, there is an abundance of fresh fish and other seafood. When I wanted shrimp, I would go down to the harbor and buy it fresh from the shrimp boats. The only problem was that all the shrimp never made it home! Serve as an hors d'oeuvre or make shrimp sandwiches on French bread.*

In a large bowl, mix the green peas, iceberg lettuce, and most of the shrimp—save some for garnishing. In another bowl, beat together sour cream, mayonnaise, gin, Tabasco sauce, catsup, lemon juice, pepper, and dill. Pour dressing over shrimp and lettuce. Mix gently. Arrange on lettuce leaves and garnish with shrimp and lemon slices.

– Serves 4 –

# Potato Salad
[Potet Salat]

Boil potatoes and cut into cubes. Cut peeled apples, celery, and onions into small pieces and combine with potatoes in large bowl.

DRESSING

Mix the dressing ingredients together and pour over vegetables and fruit. Gently fold together until well blended. Chill before serving. This potato salad tastes best the next day.

– SERVES 6 –

8 POTATOES

2 APPLES

4 CELERY STALKS

8 GREEN ONIONS

DRESSING

½ CUP MAYONNAISE

½ CUP SOUR CREAM

2 TEASPOONS STONE GROUND MUSTARD

1 TEASPOON COARSELY GROUND PEPPER

1 TEASPOON SALT

¼ POUND SALAMI IN SLICES

¼ POUND HAM IN SLICES

1 6-OUNCE JAR GREEN OLIVES

2 ORANGES

1 BOX TOOTHPICKS

## Salami and Ham on an Orange

[Appelsin med Sinke og Pølse]

Roll the salami and ham slices and stick them on toothpicks with olives. Cut a slice off the bottom of the oranges and place on serving tray. Insert the toothpicks into the oranges until completely covered.

– SERVES 6 –

Selg ikke skinnet før bjørnen er skutt.

*Don't sell the fur before the bear is shot.*

## Mustard Sauce for Roast Beef

[Seneps Saus med Kald Biff]

Stir ingredients together in a small bowl. Arrange cold roast beef slices on serving platter around the bowl of sauce and garnish with radishes and parsley.

– SERVES 6 –

¼ CUP MAYONNAISE

3 TABLESPOONS SOUR CREAM

2 TEASPOONS STONE GROUND MUSTARD

¼ TEASPOON HORSERADISH

¼ TEASPOON PEPPER

¼ TEASPOON SALT

1 POUND COLD ROAST BEEF, SLICED

# *Aquavit*
## [Akvavit]

Serve aquavit in shot glasses, ice cold and straight from the freezer. It is most often served with dinner and used for toasts. But beware, aquavit has a big bite—more than four toasts and you'll regret it in the morning.

Aquavit is matured in oak barrels and put on board ships for trips across the equator. The rolling action of the ocean combined with the change in temperature give this drink its smoothness. The inside of the label identifies on which ship it sailed and how many trips it made across the equator.

# Potatoes and Carrots in Parsley Sauce

[Poteter og Gulrøtter i Persille Saus]

Peel and quarter the potatoes and carrots. Boil in salted water until almost soft, about 20 minutes. Remove from water and cut into bite-sized pieces.

While vegetables are cooking, melt the butter in a pan and add flour. Stir. Slowly add milk while beating with a wire whisk until all milk is used. Let sauce simmer over low heat, stirring constantly, until ready to boil. Add parsley, salt, and pepper and remove from heat.

Place vegetables in serving dish and pour sauce over all. Serve immediately.

– SERVES 4 –

6 POTATOES

4 CARROTS

2 TABLESPOONS BUTTER

2 TABLESPOONS FLOUR

2 CUPS MILK

4 TABLESPOONS CHOPPED PARSLEY

SALT AND PEPPER TO TASTE

½ head Iceberg Lettuce

2 hard-boiled Eggs

½ Cucumber

1 Red Pepper

2 Tomatoes

¼ cup Green Olives

DRESSING

½ cup Olive Oil

¼ cup Cider Vinegar

1 teaspoon Tarragon

1 clove Garlic, crushed

Salt and Pepper to taste

# *May Salad*
## [Mai Salat]

Tear lettuce into small pieces and cut or slice eggs and vegetables. Combine in a large mixing bowl and set aside.

DRESSING

Combine ingredients in jar with lid and shake well. Pour over salad and toss. Serve immediately.

– Serves 4 –

# Crumb Cake with Cream
## [Krumkaker med Krem]

Beat eggs and sugar stiff with an electric beater. Add melted butter, cardamom, and flour and beat some more. (Add 1 to 3 tablespoons water if batter seems too thick.) Grease the krumkake iron and heat until hot. Pour a little batter into the krumkake iron and cook until krumkake is golden yellow. Remove immediately and wrap around the krumkake pinne. You'll have to do this very quickly before the krumkake has a chance to cool; it is most pliable while still warm. Repeat process until batter is gone. Set krumkakes aside and prepare filling.

## FILLING
Whip cream until stiff and prepare fruit. Fill krumkake cones with berries and/or ice cream. Top with whipped cream.

– Makes 16 to 20 –

3 Eggs

1 cup Sugar

¾ cup melted Butter

1 teaspoon Cardamom or
    Vanilla

2 cups Flour

FILLING

1 pint Heavy Cream

4 cups Fresh Berries
    of your choice

Ice Cream (optional)

*NOTE: You will need a krumkake iron and a krumkake pinne for this recipe, both of which are available at kitchen and/or Scandinavian specialty stores. The iron is similar to a waffle iron; the pinne is used to shape the krumkaker into cones. Once prepared, krumkakers store well in an airtight container.*

# June

## [Juni]

### BREAKFAST

WAFFLES

### LUNCH

CHICKEN SALAD

SESAME SEED ROLLS

APPLE-RHUBARB PIE

### DINNER

SISTER VERONICA'S SPINACH TARTS

BOILED POTATOES

OVEN-BAKED FLOUNDER

SUMMER VEGETABLES

STRAWBERRY SHORTCAKE

# Waffles
## [Fløtevafler]

*This is my family's favorite breakfast. If you use an electric waffle iron, place it on the table and prepare them while you eat. Waffles are also good cold with fruit, jam, and/or honey.*

Crack eggs into a large bowl. Add sugar and cardamom and beat with an electric mixer for three minutes. Sprinkle in the flour, baking powder, and salt. Add sour cream and butter. Beat until batter is smooth. Let batter sit for 20 minutes.

Warm waffle iron until hot and melt ½ teaspoon butter or margarine in the iron before you pour ¼ cup batter into the center. The waffles are ready when they are light brown. Serve warm with whipped cream and fresh strawberries or a topping of your choice.

– MAKES 10 WAFFLES –

6 EGGS

½ CUP SUGAR

1 TEASPOON GROUND CARDAMOM

1½ CUPS FLOUR

1 TEASPOON BAKING POWDER

PINCH SALT

1 CUP SOUR CREAM

½ CUP MELTED BUTTER

3 TABLESPOONS MARGARINE OR BUTTER FOR FRYING

1 PINT HEAVY CREAM

1 PINT FRESH STRAWBERRIES

# Chicken Salad
## [Kylling Salat]

*This dish is light and juicy—perfect for a summer meal.*

Preheat oven to 350°. Rub chicken with salt and roast in the oven for 1½ hours. After cooking, let cool long enough to allow for easy handling, about 20 minutes. Bone the chicken and cut the meat into bite-sized pieces.

Peel and cut apples and orange and combine with halved grapes, pineapple bits, and chicken in a large mixing bowl. Add sour cream, mayonnaise, and pepper. Arrange the chicken salad on a bed of lettuce and chill well before serving. Keeps in the refrigerator for 3 days.

– SERVES 6 –

1 MEDIUM CHICKEN

1 TEASPOON SALT

2 APPLES

1 ORANGE

1 CUP GREEN GRAPES

1 CUP DRAINED PINEAPPLE BITS

1 CUP SOUR CREAM

¾ CUP MAYONNAISE

1 TEASPOON COARSELY GROUND PEPPER

1 HEAD LETTUCE

¼ POUND BUTTER

2¼ CUPS MILK

1 PACKAGE YEAST

1 TEASPOON SUGAR

8 CUPS FLOUR

1 TEASPOON SALT

1 EGG, BEATEN

2 TEASPOONS SESAME SEEDS

# Sesame Seed Rolls
## [Rundstykker med Frø]

*I call these "Sunday rolls" because I make them Saturday night and let them rise overnight so they're ready to bake Sunday morning. They freeze well in an airtight bag.*

In a saucepan, melt the butter, warm the milk, and let cool to body temperature. Add yeast and sugar and stir until dissolved. Add most of the flour and all of the salt. Knead until dough is smooth. Cover the dough and set aside in a warm place for 30 minutes.

Knead the dough some more and divide into egg-sized rolls. Place on a cookie sheet and brush with beaten egg. Sprinkle with sesame seeds. Cover the rolls and allow to rise for an additional 2 hours (or overnight). Bake for 20 minutes at 350°.

– MAKES 20 ROLLS –

# Apple-Rhubarb Pie
## [Eple og Rabarbra Kake]

*This dessert always makes me think of early summer in Norway when the days never end.*

In a bowl, combine flour, crumbled butter, and egg. Knead until smooth. Put the dough in the refrigerator while you prepare the filling.

Peel and cut apples into wedges. Clean and cut rhubarb into small pieces and cook for five minutes in 2 tablespoons of water. Add the corn starch and sugar. Roll out the pie dough to fit a 9″ pie pan. Spoon rhubarb filling on top and arrange apple slices around. Sprinkle cinnamon over the pie and pour the honey on top. Bake at 350° until the crust is golden brown, about 30 minutes. Serve with whipped cream or vanilla ice cream.

— MAKES 1 PIE —

2 CUPS FLOUR

⅓ POUND BUTTER

1 EGG

4 APPLES

1¼ CUPS RHUBARB

2 TABLESPOONS WATER

1 TABLESPOON CORN STARCH

2 TABLESPOONS SUGAR

1 TEASPOON CINNAMON

4 TABLESPOONS HONEY

1 PINT HEAVY CREAM OR
   VANILLA ICE CREAM

## Sister Veronica's Spinach Tarts

[Søster Veronica's
Spinat Terter]

In a bowl, combine flour, salt, and egg. Knead butter in quickly and add lemon juice and water. Knead some more and refrigerate for 30 minutes.

Preheat oven to 350°. Roll the dough out to $\frac{1}{6}$″ thick and lift it over the tart or muffin tins. Roll over the tartlets, cutting the dough. Form the dough with your thumb to fit the tins. Poke holes in the bottom with a fork. Bake for 8 minutes or until golden brown.

### FILLING

Melt butter in a pan over low heat. Add flour and keep stirring. Add half-and-half until sauce is thick. Stir in ham, mushrooms, and spinach. Salt and pepper to taste. Fill the tart shells and decorate with parsley. Serve warm.

– SERVES 8 –

1½ CUPS FLOUR

¼ TEASPOON SALT

1 EGG

½ CUP BUTTER

2 TABLESPOONS LEMON JUICE

2 TABLESPOONS COLD WATER

FILLING

2 TABLESPOONS BUTTER

2 TABLESPOONS FLOUR

1 CUP HALF & HALF

1 CUP CHOPPED, COOKED HAM

1 CUP MUSHROOMS, SLICED AND SAUTÉED

1 PACKAGE FROZEN SPINACH, DEFROSTED, DRAINED, AND CHOPPED

SALT AND PEPPER TO TASTE

A FEW SPRIGS PARSLEY

# Boiled Potatoes

[Kokte Poteter]

8 Potatoes

Water to cover potatoes

1 teaspoon Salt

4 tablespoons chopped Parsley

Peel potatoes and cut largest ones into quarters. Boil in salted water for 40 minutes, or until soft. Serve in a hot serving dish sprinkled with chopped parsley.

– Serves 4 –

# Oven-Baked Flounder
## [Gratinert Flyndre]

*Norwegians have a thousand different methods for preparing fish, but this recipe is one of the best. Even people who don't usually like fish enjoy this dish.*

Preheat oven to 350°. Grease a shallow baking dish and place the fish in it. Sprinkle with salt and pepper. Spoon the lemon juice over the fish.

In a pot, melt butter or margarine. Stir in flour. Add half-and-half and stir until thick. Remove from heat and cool slightly, then beat in eggs.

Pour sauce over the fish and sprinkle with Parmesan cheese. Bake at 350° for 30 minutes or until golden brown.

— SERVES 4 —

2 POUNDS FLOUNDER

½ TEASPOON FRESHLY GROUND PEPPER

½ TEASPOON SALT

JUICE OF ONE LEMON

2 TABLESPOONS BUTTER OR MARGARINE

3 TABLESPOONS FLOUR

1½ CUPS HALF & HALF

2 EGGS

½ CUP GRATED PARMESAN

*NOTE: For a fancier dinner, add ½ pound shelled shrimp to top of the fish before adding the sauce.*

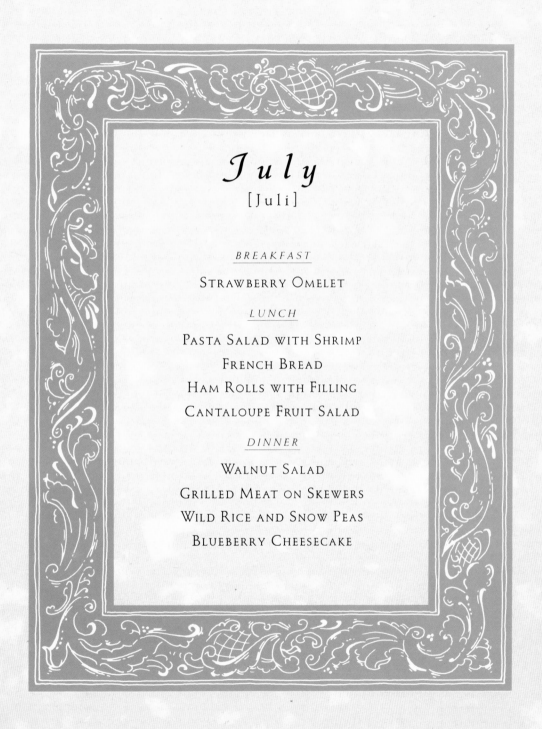

# *July*
## [Juli]

Strawberry Omelet

*LUNCH*

Pasta Salad with Shrimp

French Bread

Ham Rolls with Filling

Cantaloupe Fruit Salad

*DINNER*

Walnut Salad

Grilled Meat on Skewers

Wild Rice and Snow Peas

Blueberry Cheesecake

# Strawberry Omelet
## [Jordbær Omeleft]

*An inviting meal for breakfast or lunch.*

Beat the eggs in a mixing bowl with the orange liqueur or juice. Clean and slice the strawberries (if you use frozen, defrost and drain); set aside. Melt the butter in a skillet over low heat. Pour omelet batter into the skillet. Add half the sliced strawberries to the omelet and cover with a lid. The omelet will be done when the eggs are set. Fold the omelet in half and arrange it on a plate with the rest of the strawberries and orange slices. Sprinkle honey or powdered sugar over the omelet and serve immediately.

– SERVES 1 –

2 EGGS

2 TABLESPOONS ORANGE LIQUEUR OR ORANGE JUICE

15 FRESH STRAWBERRIES

1 TEASPOON BUTTER

2 TABLESPOONS POWDERED SUGAR OR HONEY

2 ORANGE SLICES FOR GARNISH

# Pasta Salad with Shrimp

[Kald Makaroni Salat
med Reker]

*This dish is great for hot summer days, and once you've
had it, you'll crave it again very soon.*

Boil the pasta shells according to package directions,
rinse, and drain. In a large bowl, combine the pasta,
olives, artichoke hearts, asparagus, and shrimp.

DRESSING
Combine all dressing ingredients in a separate mixing
bowl and spoon over everything; toss lightly to blend
well. Arrange the salad on a bed of greens and serve
chilled.

– SERVES 6 –

1-POUND PACKAGE PASTA SHELLS

½ CUP SLICED BLACK OR
    GREEN OLIVES

1 6-OUNCE JAR ARTICHOKE
    HEARTS, SLICED

1 CUP ASPARAGUS, COOKED AND
    CHOPPED INTO 1″ PIECES

1 POUND SHRIMP, COOKED AND
    PEELED

DRESSING

½ CUP OLIVE OIL

¼ CUP VINEGAR

½ TEASPOON CHOPPED GARLIC

½ TEASPOON PEPPER

2 TEASPOONS BASIL

1 TEASPOON SALT

2 TABLESPOONS GRATED PARMESAN

# French Bread
## [Loff]

*This is an easy way to make french bread.*

Preheat oven to 350°. Dissolve the yeast in warm water. Add the flour and salt. Knead for 15 minutes until dough is smooth. Cover with towel and let rise for 2 hours.

Divide dough into four parts and lay sections on a baking sheet. Cover with a damp tea towel. Let the loaves rise for an additional 1½ hours. After rising, remove towel and carefully brush the loaves with beaten egg. With a sharp knife, slit each loaf on top four times. Place a pan of water in the oven and put the baking sheet above it. Bake for about 15 minutes.

– MAKES 4 LOAVES –

1 PACKAGE YEAST

¾ CUP WARM WATER

4 CUPS FLOUR

2 TEASPOONS SALT

1 EGG FOR GLAZE

## Ham Rolls with Filling

[Sinke med Fyll]

20 slices cooked Ham

2 Carrots, cleaned and
grated

1 cup shredded
White Cabbage

½ cup Mayonnaise

3 teaspoons Heavy Cream

¼ cup Sour Cream

Salt to taste

14 Green or Black Olives

*This recipe can also be used as an appetizer and is very easy to make.*

Cut six slices of ham into small bits. In a bowl, combine the ham, carrots, cabbage, mayonnaise, cream, and sour cream. Salt to taste. On each of the remaining slices of ham, spread a spoonful of filling over the middle and roll. Stick a toothpick with an olive on it through the roll to hold it together.

– Serves 6 –

Rullende sten samler ikke mose.

*Rolling stones do not gather moss.*

# Cantaloupe Fruit Salad
## [Melon Frukt Salat]

Cut the cantaloupes in half and remove the seeds. Scoop out most of the meat with a melon baller or spoon and mix with the other fruit and sugar. Spoon the lemon juice and brandy over the fruit mixture. Cover and chill.

Before serving, spoon the fruit salad into the hollow melons and garnish with fresh mint leaves. Ice cream is also very good with this salad.

– SERVES 6 –

3 SMALL CANTALOUPES

1½ POUNDS MIXED FRUIT, IN SEASON (I LIKE TO USE RASPBERRIES, STRAWBERRIES, KIWI, GRAPES, AND APPLES)

¾ CUP SUGAR

JUICE OF ONE LEMON

½ CUP APRICOT BRANDY

FRESH MINT LEAVES FOR GARNISH

Et eple om dagen er godf for magen.
*An apple a day is good for the stomach.*

# Walnut Salad
## [Valnøtt Salat]

*This is a refreshing salad for a hot summer day.*

Preheat oven to 350°. Sprinkle walnuts onto a baking sheet and toast for 5 minutes.

Prepare spinach, peas, mushrooms, and grapefruit as directed and toss in large mixing bowl.

DRESSING

In separate container, combine ingredients for dressing, mix well, and spoon over salad. Add walnuts and serve.

– SERVES 6 –

¼ CUP WALNUTS

3 CUPS SPINACH OR
   ICEBERG LETTUCE, SLICED

2 CUPS SUGAR PEAS

½ CUP SLICED MUSHROOMS

1 GRAPEFRUIT, PEELED AND CUT
   INTO BITE-SIZED PIECES

DRESSING

½ CUP OLIVE OIL

4 TABLESPOONS APPLE CIDER OR
   OTHER FRUIT VINEGAR

SALT AND FRESHLY GROUND
   PEPPER

## Grilled Meat on Skewers
[ G r i l l   K j ø t t   P å   P i n n e ]

2 POUNDS LAMB OR BEEF

2 CUPS BEER

½ CUP OLIVE OIL

1 CUP WATER

1 TABLESPOON OREGANO

1 TEASPOON ROSEMARY

1 TEASPOON PEPPER

1 BAY LEAF CRUMBLED

1 GREEN PEPPER, CUBED

1 ONION, WEDGED

1 TOMATO, WEDGED

12 OUNCES MUSHROOMS, WHOLE

1 LEMON

*With marinated lamb, this recipe is my dad's favorite. It's fun to eat and easy to prepare.*

Cut the meat into cubes and place in a bowl. Add liquids and spices to cubes. Cover and refrigerate for 8 hours or overnight.

Arrange the meat alternately with the vegetables on skewers. Return the meat and vegetable skewers to the marinade until you are ready to grill. Cook on a hot grill about 8 minutes on each side. Squeeze lemon over the meat before serving.

– SERVES 6 –

# Wild Rice and Snow Peas
## [Vill Ris og Erter]

*Vary this recipe by substituting mushrooms—or other vegetables, nuts, or fruits—for the snow peas.*

Rinse the wild and white rice. Melt butter in an iron skillet. Stir in onions and cook until soft. Add the rice, water, bouillon, salt, pepper, cumin, piñon nuts, and rosemary. Simmer over low heat for 50 minutes. Add snow peas. Cook for 5 minutes longer. Pour into serving bowl and sprinkle with parsley. Serve immediately.

— SERVES 6 TO 8 —

1 CUP WILD RICE

1 CUP WHITE, LONG-GRAIN RICE

5 TEASPOONS BUTTER

½ CUP CHOPPED ONION

4¼ CUPS WATER

2 BEEF BOUILLON CUBES

½ TEASPOON SALT

PEPPER TO TASTE

½ TEASPOON CUMIN

½ CUP PIÑON NUTS

½ TEASPOON ROSEMARY, CRUSHED

1 CUP CUT SNOW PEAS

3 TABLESPOONS PARSLEY

2 8-OUNCE PACKAGES
CREAM CHEESE

1½ CUPS SUGAR

2 TABLESPOONS LEMON JUICE

5 EGGS

2 CUPS SOUR CREAM

2 TEASPOONS VANILLA

2 TABLESPOONS CORN STARCH

2 CUPS GRAHAM CRACKER
CRUMBS

5 TABLESPOONS BLUEBERRIES
OR JAM

2 CUPS FRESH BLUEBERRIES OR
BLUEBERRY JAM

1 CUP WHIPPING CREAM,
WHIPPED STIFF

# Blueberry Cheesecake
## [Kremkake med Blåbær]

Preheat oven to 350°. In a mixing bowl, beat cream cheese with sugar and lemon juice until soft and well mixed. Add to this mixture the eggs, sour cream, vanilla, and corn starch. Beat until well blended.

Crush graham crackers with rolling pin. Grease a 9″ spring pan or tall pie pan. Sprinkle the crumbs evenly over the bottom of the pan. Pour half the batter onto the crumbs and sprinkle with 5 tablespoons blueberries or jam. Pour remaining batter over blueberries. Put the cheesecake into a water bath (a larger pan filled with water). Bake at 350° for 1 hour. Turn the oven off and allow the cheesecake to sit in the oven for another hour. Cool and decorate with fresh blueberries or jam and whipped cream.

– MAKES 1 CHEESECAKE –

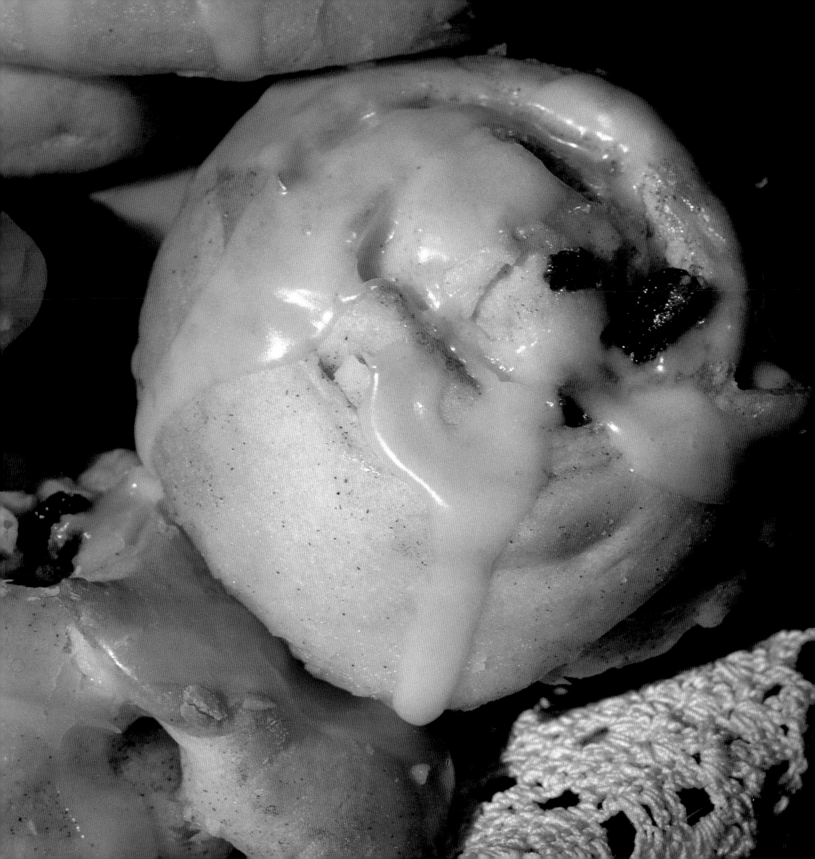

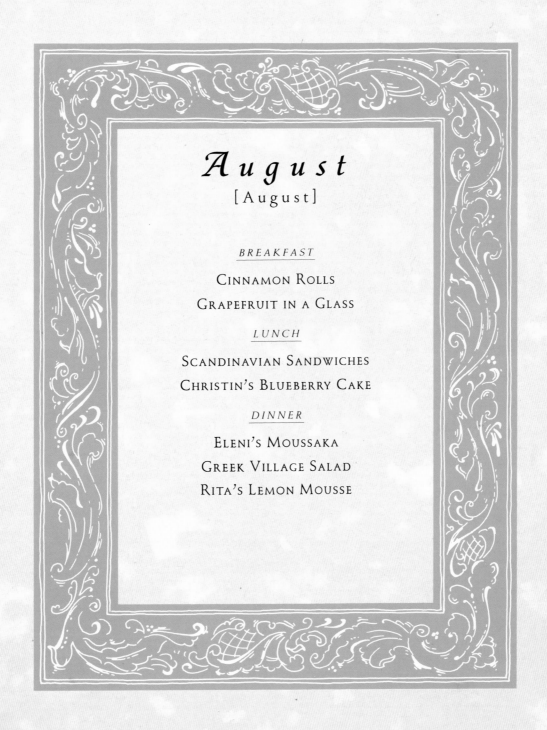

# *August*

[August]

*BREAKFAST*

Cinnamon Rolls

Grapefruit in a Glass

*LUNCH*

Scandinavian Sandwiches

Christin's Blueberry Cake

*DINNER*

Eleni's Moussaka

Greek Village Salad

Rita's Lemon Mousse

# Cinnamon Rolls
[ K a n e l k a k e r ]

*The aroma of these cinnamon rolls should get your family up in a hurry.*

Dissolve yeast in warm water and combine in a small bowl with sugar, vanilla, and beaten egg. Stir well. In a large bowl, combine the yeast mixture with flour and cardamom. Mix well. Knead together quickly and add butter. Knead quickly by squeezing with your fingers. Work the dough until the butter has been absorbed into it. This needs to be done quickly so the butter does not become too soft and make the dough slimey. Place the dough on the top shelf of the refrigerator for 1 hour until well cooled.

## FILLING

Roll dough into a large rectangle with rolling pin and spread butter over dough. Sprinkle with cinnamon, sugar, and raisins. Roll dough sideways until you

1 PACKAGE YEAST

½ CUP WARM WATER

2 TABLESPOONS SUGAR

1 TEASPOON VANILLA

1 EGG, BEATEN

3 CUPS FLOUR

¼ TEASPOON CARDAMOM

½ POUND BUTTER, ROOM
  TEMPERATURE

FILLING

4 TEASPOONS BUTTER, ROOM
  TEMPERATURE

2 TABLESPOONS CINNAMON

2 TABLESPOONS SUGAR

1 CUP RAISINS

1 EGG WHITE

FROSTING

1 CUP POWDERED SUGAR

A LITTLE LEMON JUICE

*NOTE: This recipe can also be used to make Princess Cake: arrange the rolls in a circle around one in the middle and sprinkle with slivered almonds before baking.*

have a long roll. Cut the roll into slices and lay each slice face down on a greased baking sheet. Press each one slightly with your hand. Cover with a damp tea towel and let rise in a warm place for 2 hours or in a cooler place overnight. Pencil each roll with a little egg white and bake at 350° for 10 to 15 minutes or until golden brown. Let cool slightly before frosting.

FROSTING

In a mixing bowl, add the lemon juice to the powdered sugar a little at a time until the mixture has a honey-like consistency. Pour over cinnamon rolls or princess cake.

– SERVES 6 –

# Scandinavian Sandwiches
## [Smørbrød]

*Here is a list of all the ingredients I have used in my sandwiches with some possible combinations and arrangements pictured. The best results, however, come when you have fun creating these colorful sandwiches. You don't need much of each ingredient, so this is an elegant and inexpensive way to serve an impressionable lunch.*

*BREAD*

DANISH RYE BREAD

FRENCH BREAD

*CONDIMENTS*

BUTTER

MAYONNAISE

MUSTARD

*FISH*

HERRING

SMOKED SALMON

SHRIMP

*MEAT*

SALAMI

ROAST BEEF

LIVER PÂTÉ

BACON

ROAST PORK

*EGGS*

COOKED EGGS

### *FRUITS AND VEGETABLES*

| | |
|---|---|
| Onions | Beets |
| Cucumbers | Lemons |
| Pickles | Tomatoes |
| Lettuce | Olives |
| Parsley | Radishes |
| Oranges | Potatoes |

### *CHEESE*

Norwegian Goat Cheese

Jarlsburg

Blue Cheese

Camembert

### *SPICES*

Salt

Pepper

Chives

Dill

# Christin's Blueberry Cake
[Blåbærkake]

*This blueberry cake is a favorite. It is usually gone before it has a chance to cool.*

Preheat oven to 350°. Beat butter and sugar until blended. Add vanilla, eggs, and sour cream and beat some more. In a separate bowl, combine flour, baking powder, baking soda, and cardamom. Mix well. Add flour mixture to liquid mixture a little at a time. When the batter is thick, it is ready.

Pour half the batter into a 9″ spring form (use a larger one for a wider cake). Sprinkle the blueberries on top of the batter then sprinkle with cinnamon. Pour remaining batter over the blueberries and cinnamon. Bake at 350° for 45 minutes. Poke the cake with a toothpick to see if it is done (toothpick should come out clean). If not, let it stay in a little longer. When cooled, dust the cake with powdered sugar.

– MAKES 1 CAKE –

⅓ POUND BUTTER, ROOM TEMPERATURE

1 CUP SUGAR

2 TEASPOONS VANILLA

4 EGGS

1 CUP SOUR CREAM

3 CUPS FLOUR

1 TEASPOON BAKING POWDER

1 TEASPOON BAKING SODA

¼ TEASPOON CARDAMOM

2 CUPS BLUEBERRIES, FRESH OR FROZEN

2 TEASPOONS CINNAMON

1 CUP POWDERED SUGAR

# Eleni's Moussaka

*I learned to make this dish while living in Greece. The old fisherman's wife next door wanted to marry me to one of her eligible bachelor nephews. Because of this, she thought I should know how to cook Greek food. I learned to cook some wonderful Greek food but, to her disappointment, never married one of her nephews.*

Cut eggplants into slices and soak in water for 30 minutes to remove bitterness. Dry with paper towels. Turn the eggplant in flour and fry in olive oil until brown on both sides. Put the fried slices on paper towels to remove excess grease.

In a hot frying pan, stir the ground meat with spices, tomatoes, and onion until meat is cooked. Add the tomato paste and a little water. Simmer on low heat for 20 minutes.

2 Eggplants

4 tablespoons Flour

Olive Oil for frying

1½ pounds ground Lamb or Beef

1 teaspoon Salt

½ teaspoon Pepper

1 Bay Leaf

1 teaspoon Oregano

¼ teaspoon Cinnamon

½ teaspoon Cumin

2 tablespoons chopped Parsley

2 large Tomatoes

1 Onion, cut into small bits

4 tablespoons Tomato Paste

SAUCE

5 tablespoons Margarine

5 tablespoons Flour

2½ cups Milk

3 Egg Yolks

2 whole Eggs

1 cup Cefalotire or
Parmesan Cheese, grated

SAUCE

Melt margarine in a pan and add flour. Stir. Add milk a little at a time while beating with a wire whisk until sauce becomes a thick, even white sauce. Turn heat off and beat egg yolks into the sauce. Add whole eggs. Add the grated cheese less ¼ cup, which is reserved for the top.

In an oven-proof dish, arrange a layer of eggplant and a layer of meat mixture. Repeat until all ingredients are used. Pour cheese sauce over the top. Sprinkle with grated cheese and bake at 375° until golden brown, about 45 minutes. Let moussaka cool a bit before serving.

– Serves 6 –

# Greek Village Salad
## [Gresk Landsby Salat]

*In Greece, this is called horjatiki salad, which means village salad. The Greeks use what is available, such as watercress or radishes, but I have never had a horjatiki salad without feta, olives, or tomatoes. This salad is a meal in itself.*

In a large salad bowl, combine lettuce, tomatoes, cucumber, cabbage, and green pepper. Toss the salad and arrange olives and feta cheese on top.

## DRESSING

Mix all ingredients together in a jar or bowl. Pour over the salad just before serving. The dressing keeps well, so make extra for other salads if you wish.

— SERVES 4 TO 6 —

½ HEAD ICEBERG OR ROMAINE LETTUCE, TORN

2 TOMATOES, CUT INTO WEDGES

1 CUCUMBER, THINLY SLICED

1 CUP CABBAGE, SHREDDED

1 GREEN PEPPER, CUT INTO THICK SLIVERS

½ CUP GREEK OLIVES

½ POUND GREEK FETA CHEESE, CUT INTO SMALL CUBES

DRESSING

¼ CUP OLIVE OIL

¼ CUP CIDER VINEGAR

1 TEASPOON OREGANO

1 CLOVE GARLIC, CRUSHED OR FINELY CHOPPED

½ TEASPOON PEPPER

# Rita's Lemon Mousse
## [Rita's Sitron Dessert]

*This dessert is tart and light—a great end to a large meal.*

Dissolve the lemon gelatin as instructed on the package but substitute 1 cup of lemon juice for 1 cup of water. Let gelatin cool and set slightly. In separate bowl, beat egg whites until stiff and fold in powdered sugar. In a third bowl, beat whipping cream. Stir and fold together the egg whites, whipped cream, and lemon gelatin. If gelatin is too stiff, put it in the blender for about 30 seconds before adding other ingredients. Pour the lemon mousse into eight separate serving dishes or glasses. Decorate with additional whipped cream, a sprig of mint, or a flower.

– SERVES 8 –

1 6-OUNCE PACKAGE
LEMON GELATIN

1 CUP LEMON JUICE

2 EGG WHITES

1 CUP POWDERED SUGAR

1 PINT HEAVY CREAM

ADDITIONAL WHIPPED CREAM
FOR TOPPING (OPTIONAL)

# September

[September]

*BREAKFAST*

Crepes with Apricot and Cream Filling

*LUNCH*

Onion Tart

Country Rye Bread

Tomato Feta Salad

Vanilla Pastries

*DINNER*

Trout Salad

Stuffed Pork Roast · Brown Sauce

Roasted Potatoes

Glazed Carrots

Whiskey Cranberries

Sour Cucumbers

Pears Deluxe

# Crepes with Apricot and Cream Filling

[Pannekaker med Aprikos og Krem]

*Crepes are quick and easy to make. The apricot and cream filling is delicious, but if you are in a hurry, jam also works great with this recipe.*

Blend flour, sugar, and salt in a bowl. Add milk and beat for 3 minutes. Let sit for 20 minutes. Add the eggs and vanilla and beat until smooth.

Warm a frying pan and melt 1 teaspoon butter in it. Add a small amount of batter and turn the pan until it is evenly coated with batter. Flip the crepe. It should be light brown on each side and very thin. Repeat until all batter is used. Fold crepes in half and store between two hot plates.

1½ cups Flour

1 teaspoon Sugar

¼ teaspoon Salt

2 cups Milk

2 Eggs

1 tablespoon Vanilla

2 tablespoons Butter
for frying

Liten tue velter stort lass.

*A little hill can tip a big load.*

APRICOT AND CREAM FILLING

1 29-OUNCE CAN APRICOTS OR
    10 FRESH APRICOTS

1 PINT HEAVY CREAM

½ CUP POWDERED SUGAR

½ CUP TOASTED ALMONDS

½ TEASPOON NUTMEG

## APRICOT AND CREAM FILLING

Keep in mind that it is almost impossible to find fresh apricots at this time of year, so canned apricots may be used. Pour the apricots in a pot and heat on low until they are warmed through. If you use fresh apricots, simmer them in a pot with 2 cups of water and ½ cup sugar for 15 minutes or until soft. Then peel and pit the fruit.

Whip the cream with ½ cup powdered sugar until stiff. Chop ½ cup almonds and sprinkle onto cookie sheet. Bake just a few minutes at 375° until slightly brown.

Fold a small portion of warm apricots into each crepe with 2 teaspoons whipped cream. Sprinkle toasted almonds and a dash of nutmeg on top of each crepe. Serve immediately.

– MAKES 12 CREPES –

# Onion Tart
## [Løk Terte]

*A variation on quiche, this recipe feeds at least 8 people and is very tasty.*

In a bowl, stir yeast in warmed milk. Add melted butter, egg, flour, and salt. Knead dough until smooth. Cover and set in a warm place for 30 minutes.

Chop onions into small pieces and fry with butter, salt, and pepper over low heat until transparent but not brown. Cool for 10 minutes. Beat eggs and add to onions. Add flour, cream, sour cream, and basil. Stir until ingredients are well blended.

Preheat oven to 375°. Roll dough to fit two small or one large greased pie form. Pour in filling, and sprinkle with caraway or chives and crumbled bacon. Bake for 45 to 60 minutes or until dough is light brown. Serve hot, but it tastes great cold, too.

– SERVES 8 –

1 PACKAGE YEAST

1½ CUPS WARM MILK

5 TABLESPOONS MELTED BUTTER

1 EGG

4 CUPS FLOUR

½ TEASPOON SALT

FILLING

9 ONIONS

5 TABLESPOONS BUTTER

½ TEASPOON SALT

¼ TEASPOON PEPPER

8 EGGS

½ CUP FLOUR

½ CUP HEAVY CREAM

1 CUP SOUR CREAM

2 TEASPOONS BASIL

8 STRIPS CRUMBLED BACON

1½ TEASPOONS CARAWAY OR CHIVES

# Country Rye Bread
## [Bonde Brød]

Pour beer and water into a pot. Heat until luke-warm. Remove ½ cup from the brew and dissolve the yeast in it. In large mixing bowl, combine beer mixture, yeast mixture, honey, melted butter, and salt. Add most of the flour to the mixture (save some for kneading). Knead until smooth.

Put the dough in a warm place and let rise for 45 minutes. Then knead for 10 minutes more and form into two loaves. Put the loaves on a baking tray and cover with a tea towel. Let rise for 2 hours and bake in preheated oven for 40 minutes at 375°.

– MAKES 2 LOAVES –

2½ CUPS BEER

¼ CUP WATER

2 PACKAGES YEAST

2 TEASPOONS HONEY

2 TEASPOONS MELTED BUTTER

1½ TEASPOON SALT

4 CUPS RYE OR
    WHOLE WHEAT FLOUR

6 CUPS FINE WHEAT FLOUR

## Stuffed Pork Roast
### [Fylt Svinekam]

5 POUNDS DEBONED PORK LOIN
(CENTER CUT)

15 PITTED PRUNES

1 APPLE, CUBED

4 TABLESPOONS CHOPPED PARSLEY

5 TABLESPOONS BUTTER

SALT AND PEPPER TO TASTE

NOTE: *Add potatoes to roasting pan after 30 minutes. See recipe page 143.*

Preheat oven to 350°. Make a deep cut, lengthwise, into the pork loin. Season inside with salt and pepper. Layer the inside of the roast with pitted prunes (soak in hot water for 30 minutes before pitting them), and apple cubes; sprinkle with parsley. Fold the roast into a roll and tie with cotton string to hold for roasting.

Melt the butter in a pot large enough to hold the roast. Brown roast on all sides. Remove the roast and put it into a roasting pan. Bake for 1½ hours. Save the drippings for brown sauce (next page).

– SERVES 6 TO 8 –

# Brown Sauce

## [Brun Saus]

Add two cups water to the roast drippings. (Keep the roast warm by wrapping in foil and a towel.) In a pot, melt the butter and stir in flour. Slowly add the drippings and water mixture. Simmer for 5 minutes, stirring constantly. Add sautéed mushrooms and salt and pepper to taste. (If the sauce is too thick, stir in a little milk or water.)

ROAST DRIPPINGS

2 CUPS WATER

2 TABLESPOONS BUTTER

2 TABLESPOONS FLOUR

1 CUP SLICED MUSHROOMS, SAUTÉED

SALT AND PEPPER

# Roasted Potatoes
## [Ovns Bakte Poteter]

16 MEDIUM POTATOES

WATER TO COVER POTATOES

1 TEASPOON CURRY

1 TEASPOON SALT

5 TABLESPOONS BUTTER

SALT AND PEPPER TO TASTE

Peel potatoes and cut in half. Bring pot of water to a boil with the salt and curry. Add potatoes, making sure they are submerged in water. Boil slowly for 15 minutes. Take the potatoes out of the water, arrange with butter in the baking pan in which you're cooking the pork roast. Sprinkle with salt and pepper. Bake potatoes next to the roast for one hour, or until golden brown.

– SERVES 8 –

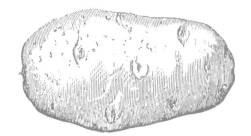

# Glazed Carrots
[Glaserte Gulrøtter]

Melt half the stick of butter in a pan and add the carrots. Stir until the carrots are coated with butter. Sprinkle with sugar and add enough water to cover the carrots. Simmer until carrots are soft, approximately 20 minutes. Melt the remaining butter over the carrots and add salt and pepper to taste.

– SERVES 8 –

¼ POUND BUTTER

1 POUND CARROTS, PEELED

1 TABLESPOON BROWN SUGAR

SALT AND PEPPER

# Whiskey Cranberries
[Tyttebær med Whiskey]

1 POUND CRANBERRIES

1 CUP SUGAR

½ CUP WHISKEY

½ CUP WATER

1½ TEASPOONS FRESHLY GROUND
    PEPPER

1 CUP SHALLOTS OR
    MEDIUM YELLOW ONION,
    CHOPPED

Put all ingredients in a pan and bring to a slow boil. Continue boiling slowly for about 25 minutes or until the cranberries begin to pop. Chill and serve.

– MAKES 2 CUPS –

# Sour Cucumbers

## [Syltede Agurker]

*This dish is very common in Scandinavia and is served with any meat dish.*

Slice the cucumber very thin. Mix the vinegar, water, sugar, salt, and pepper together in a bowl. Add cucumber slices and refrigerate for a few hours or overnight. Serve chilled or at room temperature.

– SERVES 8 –

1 CUCUMBER

½ cup WHITE VINEGAR

¼ cup WATER

2 TABLESPOONS SUGAR

1 TEASPOON SALT

1 TEASPOON PEPPER

Lite men godt sa mannen,
han patta katta.

*Little but good the man said when he nursed the cat.*

2 CUPS FLOUR

2 TEASPOONS SUGAR

1 EGG

⅓ POUND SOFTENED BUTTER

ALMOND FILLING

10 OUNCES ALMONDS

½ CUP SUGAR

½ CUP CREAM

1 TABLESPOON FLOUR

PEAR FILLING

1 28-OUNCE CAN OF PEARS

CHOCOLATE FROSTING

12 OUNCES SWEET CHOCOLATE

2 TABLESPOONS BUTTER

½ CUP STRONG COFFEE

1 PINT WHIPPED CREAM

½ CUP SLIVERED ALMONDS

# *Pears Deluxe*

[ P æ r e r  i  G o d t  S e l s k a p ]

Pour flour into a bowl and add sugar and egg. Knead in the butter until dough is smooth. Chill in the refrigerator for 15 minutes. Roll out with a rolling pin and cover the bottom of a 9″ greased spring pan.

## ALMOND FILLING

Preheat oven to 350°. Put all ingredients into a blender and grate. Pour the mixture over the dough and bake for 30 minutes.

## PEAR FILLING

Drain the pears and dry with a paper towel; arrange them on the cake.

## CHOCOLATE FROSTING

Melt the chocolate and butter in the coffee over low heat. Pour over the pears. Top with whipped cream and slivered almonds.

– SERVES 8 –

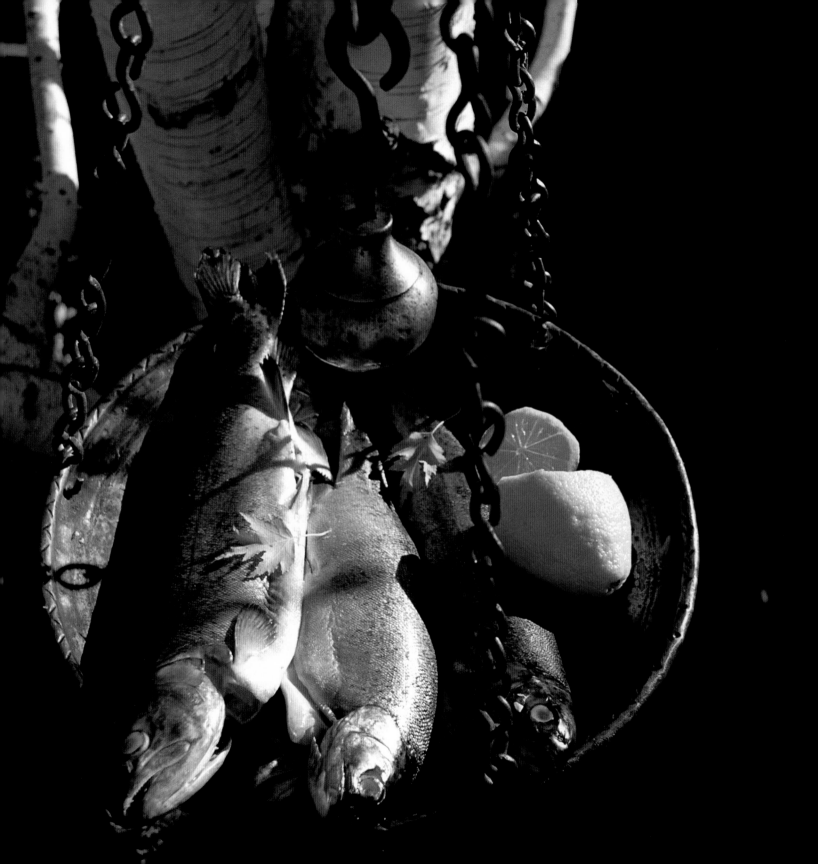

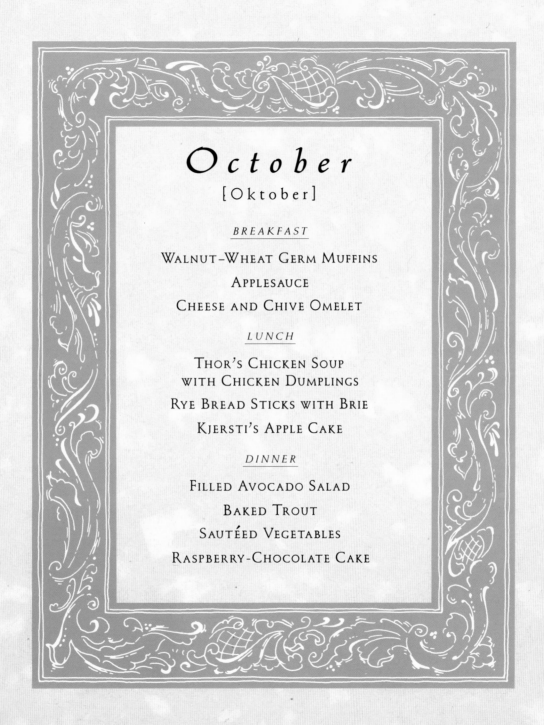

# October

## [Oktober]

### *BREAKFAST*

Walnut–Wheat Germ Muffins

Applesauce

Cheese and Chive Omelet

### *LUNCH*

Thor's Chicken Soup
with Chicken Dumplings

Rye Bread Sticks with Brie

Kjersti's Apple Cake

### *DINNER*

Filled Avocado Salad

Baked Trout

Sautéed Vegetables

Raspberry-Chocolate Cake

# Walnut–Wheat Germ Muffins
[Valnøtt Kaker]

*These muffins are easy to make. The first time I tasted them was when an English friend served me breakfast in bed. I have been hooked ever since—on the muffins and breakfast in bed. This recipe freezes well.*

Preheat oven to 350°. Beat sugar and butter until fluffy. Add the eggs, vanilla, wheat germ, flour, baking powder, baking soda, and ground walnuts. Beat the mixture for 2 minutes. Add sour cream and mix until well blended. Put the batter into muffin tins lined with paper muffin cups. Bake for 20 to 25 minutes, or until light brown and spongy.

– MAKES 24 MUFFINS –

1 CUP SUGAR

¾ CUP BUTTER, ROOM TEMPERATURE

3 EGGS

2 TEASPOONS VANILLA

½ CUP WHEAT GERM

2 CUPS ALL-PURPOSE FLOUR

1 TEASPOON BAKING POWDER

½ TEASPOON BAKING SODA

1 CUP GROUND WALNUTS

¾ CUP SOUR CREAM

# Applesauce
[Eple Saus]

*I always keep some of this applesauce in the refrigerator. It tastes great and freezes well.*

2 CUPS APPLE CIDER

1 STICK CINNAMON

4 WHOLE CLOVES

1 STRIP ORANGE PEEL

3½ POUNDS TART APPLES

¼ CUP LIGHT BROWN SUGAR

¼ CUP SUGAR

2 TEASPOONS BUTTER

In a saucepan, bring the cider to a boil. Add the spices and reduce the heat. Let simmer for 30 minutes. Remove spices. Add peeled and cut apples and sugars. Simmer for about 30 minutes. Mash the mixture with a fork and simmer for a little longer, approximately 10 minutes more. Add butter. Serve hot or cold.

– MAKES 4 CUPS –

# Cheese and Chive Omelet
[Ost og Gressløk]

Beat eggs, milk, and chives with a fork. Melt butter in pan over medium heat and add omelet mixture. Reduce heat to low. Spread cheese slices over egg mixture and cover. Cook for approximately 2 minutes or until mixture is no longer runny. Fold the omelet in half and serve immediately. Add salt and pepper to taste.

– Serves 1 –

3 Eggs

2 tablespoons Milk

1 teaspoon chopped Chives

2 teaspoons Butter

2 slices Muenster Cheese

Salt and Pepper to taste

Gammel kjærlighet rusker ikke.

*Old love does not rust.*

# Thor's Chicken Soup with Chicken Dumplings
## [Thors Kylling Suppe]

Skin chicken. Remove breast meat and set aside for use in dumplings. Put the rest of the chicken into a pot of water. Boil for 1 hour.

Prepare vegetables by cutting into bite-sized pieces. Husk corn but leave on cob (this adds a sweetness to soup).

Remove the chicken and foam from water. Add spices and vegetables and simmer soup for 15 minutes. Bone the chicken and return meat to soup. Cut corn from cob and return to soup. Discard cob. Taste soup to see if flavor is to your liking. If not, add chicken bouillon cubes for added flavor.

Prepare the dumplings and add to soup. Simmer for 10 minutes more. Serve steaming hot.

1 CHICKEN, WHOLE

12 cups WATER

8 CARROTS

6 SHALLOTS

3 stalks CELERY

4 ZUCCHINI

1 cob of CORN OR
    ½ cup frozen CORN

2 BAY LEAVES

½ teaspoon SALT

½ teaspoon PEPPER

½ teaspoon ROSEMARY

6 twigs PARSLEY

5 CHICKEN BOUILLON CUBES

CHICKEN DUMPLINGS

2 breasts of Chicken, boned
    and cut into small pieces

1 Egg

3 slices Bread

½ teaspoon Salt

¼ teaspoon Pepper

½ teaspoon Sage

1 cup Chicken Broth

## CHICKEN DUMPLINGS

In a blender, grind chicken meat. Remove from blender and combine with egg, bread, salt, pepper, and sage. Roll the mixture into marble-sized balls. Put dumplings into 1 cup boiling chicken broth for 10 minutes. Remove the dumplings and add them to the soup. (Discard the stock in which the dumplings were cooked.)

– Serves 6 –

# Rye Bread Sticks with Brie
## [Rug Stykker]

Dissolve the yeast in the warm water. Add oil, salt rye, and flour. Knead the dough until it comes off the hands and work surface. Let the dough sit, covered, in a warm place for 8 hours or longer. Then knead well and roll the dough into bread sticks. Arrange them on a floured baking pan and let rise for one hour. Place a pan of water in the oven when baking to add moisture and bake at 350° for approximately 10 minutes. Serve on decorative platter with brie.

– Makes 20 Sticks –

1 package Yeast

1½ cups warm Water

3 teaspoons Oil

2 teaspoons Salt

2½ cups Rye

1½ cups Flour

Brie Cheese

¾ POUND BUTTER, ROOM
  TEMPERATURE

1¾ CUPS SUGAR

2 TEASPOONS VANILLA

1 CUP SOUR CREAM

4 EGGS

3 CUPS FLOUR

1½ TEASPOONS BAKING POWDER

1½ TEASPOONS BAKING SODA

5 APPLES, PEELED AND CUT INTO
  WEDGES

2 TEASPOONS CINNAMON

1 CUP ALMONDS, CHOPPED

1 CUP POWDERED SUGAR

3 TEASPOONS WATER

# Kjersti's Apple Cake
[Kjersti's Eple Kake]

*This is a versatile recipe that can be made with apricots, cherries, pears, jam, or other fruit instead of apples.*

Preheat oven to 350°. Beat butter with sugar until fluffy. Add vanilla, sour cream, eggs, flour, baking powder, and baking soda. Beat until batter is smooth then pour into a greased and floured rectangular baking pan. Arrange the apple wedges in a pattern. Sprinkle with almonds and cinnamon. Bake for 45 minutes or until fork comes out clean.

Combine powdered sugar and water and pour over cake.

– SERVES 12 –

Eplet faller ikke langt fra stammen.
*The apple doesn't fall far from the tree.*

# Filled Avocado Salad
[Fylte Avocado]

Cut avocados in half and scoop out meat, leaving a small amount all around skin. Sprinkle insides with lemon juice. Chop the removed portion of avocado into bite-sized bits and mix with chopped olives, tomato, onion, lettuce, and baby corn.

DRESSING

Combine dressing ingredients in separate bowl and pour over vegetables. Mix well. Spoon into halved avocado skins and sprinkle with salt and/or freshly ground pepper.

– SERVES 4 –

2 LARGE, RIPE AVOCADOS

2 TEASPOONS LEMON JUICE

¼ CUP BLACK OLIVES, CHOPPED

1 TOMATO, CHOPPED

¼ SMALL RED ONION, CHOPPED

2 LEAVES OF LETTUCE, CHOPPED

1 16-OUNCE CAN OF BABY CORN

DRESSING

¼ CUP OLIVE OIL

2 TEASPOONS LEMON JUICE

1 CLOVE OF GARLIC, CRUSHED

SALT AND PEPPER TO TASTE

# Baked Trout

[Ø r r e t  i  O v n]

4 SMALL TROUT

4 TEASPOONS BUTTER

1 LEMON, SLICED

SALT AND PEPPER TO TASTE

1 TEASPOON DILL,
FRESH OR DRIED

*This is an easy, odor-free way to cook fish that also preserves its flavor. Serve with boiled potatoes, steamed broccoli, and fresh whole wheat bread.*

Preheat oven to 350°. Cut head from trout, open the belly with a sharp knife, and clean thoroughly with cold, salted water. Arrange each fish on a greased, square piece of foil. Put 1 tablespoon butter and a slice of lemon inside each fish. Sprinkle inside and outside of fish with salt, pepper, and dill. Fold foil into a neat package that is easy to open. Bake in oven for 20 minutes or until bones easily loosen from fish.

– SERVES 4 –

Mange bekker små blir en stor å.
*Many small streams make a big river.*

# Sautéed Vegetables
[Grønnsaker i Panne]

Clean and slice vegetables to desired sizes. In a skillet, sauté zucchini and mushrooms in butter or oil with spices until slightly soft but still crispy. In a small sauce pan, boil carrots in a cup of water until slightly soft. Drain and add carrots to zucchini. Stir while heating for a few minutes just before serving.

– SERVES 4 –

3 GREEN ZUCCHINI

3 YELLOW ZUCCHINI

¼ POUND MUSHROOMS

4 CARROTS

4 TEASPOONS BUTTER OR OIL

1 TEASPOON SAGE

½ TEASPOON ROSEMARY

SALT AND PEPPER TO TASTE

Brent barn skyr ilden.

*A burned child fears the fire.*

1 CUP WATER

4 SQUARES SEMI-SWEET
    CHOCOLATE (OR
    UNSWEETENED CHOCOLATE
    AND TWO CUPS OF SUGAR)

¼ POUND BUTTER

1 CUP SUGAR

1 CUP SOUR CREAM

2 EGGS

2 TEASPOONS VANILLA

2 CUPS FLOUR

1 TEASPOON BAKING SODA

1 TEASPOON BAKING POWDER

FILLING

1 PINT HEAVY CREAM

1 CUP POWDERED SUGAR

1½ CUPS RASPBERRIES

2 SQUARES SEMI-SWEET
    CHOCOLATE

# *Raspberry-Chocolate Cake*
## [Bringebær Sjokolade Kake]

*This cake can be made several days before serving; sprinkle cake with brandy and wrap tightly in foil. Filling can be varied.*

Preheat oven to 350°. Warm water over medium heat. Add chocolate, butter, and sugar. Set aside when chocolate and butter have melted and allow to cool for 10 minutes. Beat in sour cream, eggs, and vanilla. Add flour, baking soda, and baking powder. Beat until batter is smooth then pour into 9″ spring pan. Bake for 40 minutes or until fork comes out clean. Cool.

FILLING

Cut cooled cake into three layers. Beat cream and sugar until stiff. Spread raspberries on first layer. Use 8 tablespoons of the whipped cream mixture and spread over raspberries. Add the next layer of cake.

(continued on next page)

Melt chocolate; cool slightly. Fold melted chocolate into 1½ cups whipped cream. Spread over middle layer and add last layer of cake.

## FROSTING

Warm ingredients over low heat while stirring constantly. When frosting is smooth and still warm, spread over cake. Let cool. Put remaining whipped cream in a pastry tube and decorate cake.

– SERVES 12 –

FROSTING

4 SQUARES SEMI-SWEET CHOCOLATE

1½ CUPS POWDERED SUGAR

2 TEASPOONS RUM FLAVORING

2 TABLESPOONS BUTTER

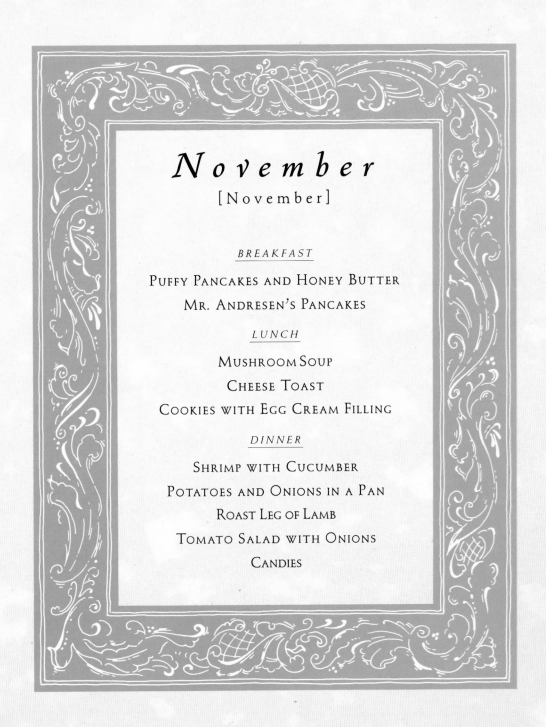

# *November*

[November]

### *BREAKFAST*

Puffy Pancakes and Honey Butter

Mr. Andresen's Pancakes

### *LUNCH*

Mushroom Soup

Cheese Toast

Cookies with Egg Cream Filling

### *DINNER*

Shrimp with Cucumber

Potatoes and Onions in a Pan

Roast Leg of Lamb

Tomato Salad with Onions

Candies

165

# Puffy Pancakes and Honey Butter

## [Tykke Pannekaker med Honning Smør]

*These can be served with syrup, jam, fruit, or berries.*

In a bowl, beat the flour, milk, egg yolks, vanilla, sugar, and baking powder until smooth. In a separate bowl, beat the egg whites until stiff. Fold the whites carefully into the first mixture. In a skillet, melt a little butter or oil and pour in ¼ cup of batter. When the pancake is slightly set and golden brown on one side, flip to the other. Keep the pancakes warm until they are ready to serve.

HONEY BUTTER

Beat the ingredients together and serve.

— SERVES 4 —

3 CUPS FLOUR

2 CUPS MILK

3 EGGS, SEPARATED

1 TEASPOON VANILLA

4 TABLESPOONS SUGAR

1 TEASPOON BAKING POWDER

BUTTER OR OIL FOR FRYING

HONEY BUTTER

½ CUP BUTTER, ROOM
    TEMPERATURE

¼ CUP HONEY

1½ CUPS FLOUR

½ TEASPOON SALT

1 TABLESPOON SUGAR

2 CUPS MILK

2 EGGS

2 TABLESPOONS BUTTER

# Mr. Andresen's Pancakes

## [Herr Andresen's Pannekaker]

*For a lighter, thinner pancake, try this recipe.*

In a bowl, mix flour, salt, and sugar. Add milk slowly while beating batter. Beat in eggs until batter is even and without lumps. Let batter sit for 30 minutes to thicken.

Melt a little butter in a frying pan and add about ¼ cup batter. Tilt frying pan to cover bottom with batter (pancakes are meant to be thin). Cook until light brown on each side. Serve with butter and powdered sugar or berries.

– SERVES 4 –

# Mushroom Soup
[S o p p   S u p p e]

*Served with cheese toast, this soup is especially tasty. It freezes well.*

In a large skillet, sauté sliced mushrooms in butter. In a pot, combine water, mushrooms, bay leaves, and chopped onion, leeks, carrots, celery, and garlic. Bring to a boil. Simmer for 30 minutes. Skim foam from top of soup and add barley and cut-up potato. Let soup simmer for another 45 minutes or until barley is tender. Season soup with dill and salt. Serve with a dollup of sour cream on top of each individual bowl.

– MAKES 12 CUPS –

1 POUND MUSHROOMS

2 TABLESPOONS BUTTER

12 CUPS WATER

3 BAY LEAVES

1 LARGE ONION

2 LEEKS

1½ CARROTS

1 CELERY ROOT

4 CLOVES OF GARLIC

1 CUP BARLEY

1 POTATO

½ TEASPOON FRESH DILL

1 TABLESPOON SALT

SOUR CREAM FOR GARNISH

## Cheese Toast
[Grillet Ost]

8 SLICES OF BREAD

2 TABLESPOONS BUTTER

4 THICK SLICES OF CHEESE

1 TOMATO, SLICED

Spread butter on one side of bread slices. Make sandwiches by putting cheese between 2 buttered slices of bread, buttered side out, and toast in a hot waffle iron or frying pan. When cheese is melted, open sandwich and insert two slices of tomato.

– SERVES 4 –

## Shrimp with Cucumber
### [Reker med Agurk]

Peel shrimp and place peelings in a pot. Add water, wine, olive oil, and shrimp and heat until shrimp turn pink. Remove shrimp and set aside. Let shrimp peelings cook for another 10 minutes then strain and discard peelings. Add cucumber and scallion strips to mixture. Let cook for two minutes and then add shrimp, mint, salt, and pepper. Warm this mixture through. Divide into 8 servings and garnish with mint.

– SERVES 8 –

1½ POUNDS MEDIUM SHRIMP

1 CUP WATER

2 TABLESPOONS WHITE WINE

¼ CUP OLIVE OIL

1 EUROPEAN CUCUMBER, CUT LENGTHWISE INTO FINE STRIPS

1 LARGE SCALLION, CUT LENGTHWISE INTO FINE STRIPS

2 TABLESPOONS MINCED MINT (FRESH IF POSSIBLE)

¾ TEASPOON SALT

¼ TEASPOON PEPPER

MINT FOR GARNISH

## Potatoes and Onions in a Pan
### [Poteter og Løk i Panne]

2 POUNDS POTATOES

6 ONIONS

2 CUPS WATER

3 TABLESPOONS PARSLEY, CHOPPED

1 TEASPOON THYME

¼ CUP MELTED BUTTER

Peel and cut potatoes and onions into 1″ thick slices and rings. Place in a roasting pan, add water, and sprinkle with parsley and thyme. Place in 350° oven for 30 minutes. Remove from oven and douse with melted butter. Cook for another 45 minutes or until potatoes are golden brown and soft.

– SERVES 8 –

# Roast Leg of Lamb
## [Lammestek]

*Lamb has been a food staple in Norway for thousands of years. My favorite way of preparing it is roasting a whole lamb on a spit over an open fire, but roast leg of lamb will do.*

Preheat oven to 350°. Rub lamb with salt, pepper, and rosemary. Cut 8 small pockets in lamb skin and insert a slice of garlic into each one. Put the lamb into a pan and roast for 2½ hours. Save drippings for gravy. If you want a pink roast, take it out earlier.

GRAVY

Pour 4 cups of water into roast drippings. In a separate pot, melt butter and brown it. Add flour and water-drippings mixture and stir with a wire whisk. Add cream, rosemary, and salt and pepper to taste. Cook for 10 minutes over low heat.

– SERVES 8 OR MORE –

3 POUND LEG OF LAMB

2 TEASPOONS SALT

1 TEASPOON PEPPER

2 TEASPOONS GROUND ROSEMARY

2 CLOVES OF GARLIC, CUT IN SLICES

GRAVY

4 CUPS WATER

ROAST DRIPPINGS

3 TABLESPOONS BUTTER

3 TABLESPOONS FLOUR

¼ CUP CREAM

1 TEASPOON ROSEMARY, CRUSHED

SALT AND PEPPER TO TASTE

# Tomato Salad with Onions
## [Tomat Salat med Løk]

Cut tomatoes into wedges and arrange in a salad bowl. Peel and cut onions and add to tomatoes. Sprinkle with parsley.

Combine dressing ingredients and whisk together. Pour over the salad and chill for two hours before serving.

– SERVES 8 –

6 TOMATOES

2 ONIONS

2 TABLESPOONS PARSLEY

DRESSING

¼ CUP OLIVE OIL

3 TABLESPOONS CIDER VINEGAR

1 TABLESPOON MUSTARD

1 TEASPOON CRUSHED GARLIC

¼ TEASPOON SALT

¼ TEASPOON PEPPER

3 CUPS POWDERED SUGAR

3 CUPS SHREDDED COCONUT

6 TABLESPOONS COCOA

2 TABLESPOONS COGNAC

1 EGG

¾ CUP BUTTER, ROOM TEMPERATURE

1 TEASPOON VANILLA

2 CUPS SHREDDED COCONUT

# Coconut Balls

[Kokos Kuler]

Stir all ingredients, except decorating coconut, together. Set mixture in refrigerator for 1 hour. After an hour, remove dough and form into little balls. Roll them in shredded coconut. Store leftovers in the refrigerator until Christmas.

– MAKES 50 CANDIES –

*Young Christin with her father in Norway.*

# Almond Tops
[Mandel Boller]

Put almond slivers on baking tray and sprinkle with powdered sugar. Bake at 375° about 10 minutes until light brown. Let cool.

Melt chocolate in a double boiler. When melted, quickly stir in almonds. Using two teaspoons, make small mounds and place on wax paper to set.

— Makes 25 Candies —

3 cups slivered Almonds

1 cup Powdered Sugar

12 ounces Sweet Chocolate

# Hazelnut Clusters
[Nøtte Topper]

Melt chocolate in a double boiler. When melted, add nuts and form small clusters using two teaspoons. Arrange clusters on wax paper and let set for 15 minutes.

— Makes 25 Candies —

12 ounces Sweet Chocolate

4 cups whole Hazelnuts

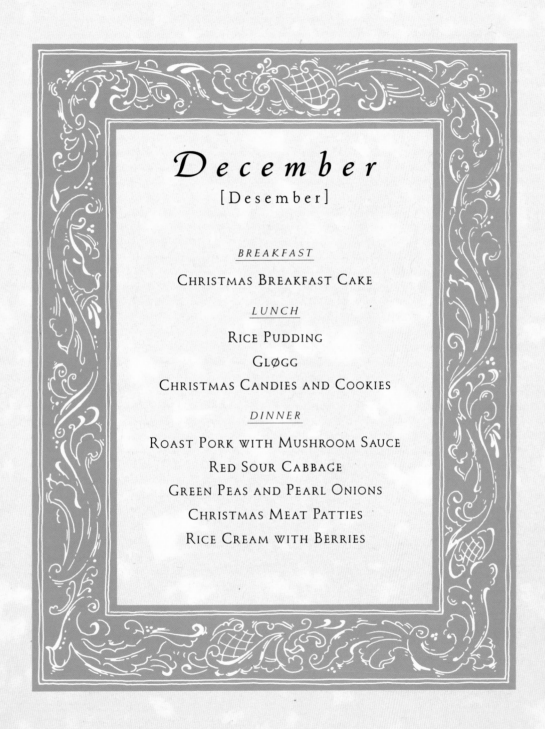

# December
## [Desember]

*BREAKFAST*

Christmas Breakfast Cake

*LUNCH*

Rice Pudding

Gløgg

Christmas Candies and Cookies

*DINNER*

Roast Pork with Mushroom Sauce

Red Sour Cabbage

Green Peas and Pearl Onions

Christmas Meat Patties

Rice Cream with Berries

# Christmas Breakfast Cake
## [Jule Kake]

*Christmas Eve breakfasts are usually kept simple because of all the other preparations that take place that day. I set the food out and let the family eat when they want to. Prepare this cake and some boiled eggs, then serve with jams and gourmet cheeses.*

Combine flour and butter. Add sugar and cardamom. Mix well. In a separate bowl, stir yeast into milk until dissolved. Beat in egg. Set dough aside and let rise until doubled (about an hour).

Knead the raisins into dough. Cut dough into two parts and form into loaves. Place in bread forms. (Take part of the dough and make a braid that fits around the top of each loaf to make them look more festive.) Let bread rise for 3 hours. Brush on beaten egg and bake at 350° for 45 minutes.

– MAKES 2 LOAVES –

7½ CUPS FLOUR

½ POUND BUTTER

½ CUP SUGAR

1 TEASPOON CARDAMOM

1 PACKAGE YEAST

2 CUPS WARM MILK

1 EGG

1 CUP RAISINS

1 EGG FOR VARNISH

# Steve's Gløgg
[Steve's Gløgg]

*This is the right prescription to liven up a dull party, and it smells so good!*

In a glass jar or pot, mix together all ingredients except aquavit, sugar, and almonds. Cover and let mixture set overnight in a cool place. (This allows the spices to develop.) Before serving, warm over low heat and stir in aquavit, sugar, and almonds. Serve in a cup with a spoon.

– SERVES 10 –

2 BOTTLES RED WINE

1 PINT SWEET VERMOUTH

2 CUPS RAISINS

1 ORANGE FOR PEEL ONLY

15 WHOLE CARDAMOMS, CRUSHED

12 WHOLE CLOVES

1 SMALL PIECE OF GINGER

2 CUPS AQUAVIT OR BRANDY

1½ CUPS BROWN SUGAR

2 CUPS ALMONDS, BLANCHED AND SLIVERED

1 Orange for peel only

1 quart Apple Cider

2 cups Cranberry Juice

¼ cup Sugar

1 Cinnamon Stick

5 whole Cloves

½ cup Raisins

# Gløgg for Children
[Gløgg får Barna]

*Gløgg is a traditional Norwegian Christmas drink. Most families have secret recipes—these can be yours!*

Cut peel from orange and combine with all other ingredients. Let mixture set in a cool place overnight or for at least 6 hours. Before serving, simmer gløgg for 30 minutes and serve warm.

– Serves 5 –

# Rice Pudding
## [ Risen Gryns Grøt ]

Bring water, salt, and cinnamon stick to a boil. Add rice. Turn heat to low and simmer for 15 minutes. Add milk and bring to a boil again. Turn off heat and cover with lid. Let rice sit for 45 minutes. Taste to see if rice is soft and has absorbed liquids. If not, bring to a slow boil again, stir, and turn off heat.

– SERVES 8 –

4 CUPS WATER

1 TEASPOON SALT

1 CINNAMON STICK

2¼ CUPS SHORT RICE

9 CUPS MILK

2 EGG YOLKS, COOKED

2 EGG YOLKS, RAW

1 CUP SUGAR

4½ CUPS FLOUR

¾ POUND SOFTENED BUTTER

2 EGG WHITES

ROUGH SUGAR FOR DIPPING

# Christmas Wreaths
## [Berliner Kranser]

Boil two eggs for 8 minutes. Take yolks out and mash with raw egg yolks. Beat in sugar and add alternately the flour and softened butter. Cool dough in refrigerator for 2 hours.

Preheat oven to 350°. Remove dough from refrigerator and form small portions into little wreaths with hands or cookie press. Arrange on cookie sheet and put in a cold place for 20 minutes. Brush wreaths with egg white and dip in sugar. Bake 10 minutes.

– MAKES 4 DOZEN COOKIES –

# *Farmboy Cookies*
## [ Trull ]

Beat sour cream with sugar. Stir in flour, water, and cardamom. Warm krumkake iron and grease it with a little butter on both sides. Put one teaspoon batter in the middle. Press iron together. Fry until trull is golden in color. Roll trull together while it is in the iron. If the cookies get too thick, add a little water to batter. Store in an airtight container.

– MAKES 1½ DOZEN COOKIES –

1¼ CUPS SOUR CREAM

¼ CUP SUGAR

1¾ CUPS FLOUR

½ CUP WATER

¼ TEASPOON CARDAMOM

BUTTER FOR THE IRON

*NOTE: You will need a krumkake iron for this recipe.*

1 EGG

¾ CUP SUGAR

2½ CUPS FLOUR

2¼ TEASPOONS BAKING POWDER

¾ CUP SOFTENED BUTTER

1 EGG WHITE

1 TABLESPOON CINNAMON

¼ CUP CHOPPED ALMONDS

2 TABLESPOONS ROUGH SUGAR

# Gros Cookies
[Gros Kjeks]

*You can make these cookies into any shape. I use circles and Christmas trees at this time of year. Prepare the same recipe in the summer and make flower shapes decorated with yellow sprinkles.*

Whip the egg and sugar until stiff. Add flour and baking powder alternately with the softened butter. Place dough in refrigerator for 1 hour.

Preheat oven to 350°. Roll dough out to ¼″ thick. Cut desired shapes with cookie cutters. Place cookies on greased baking tray. Brush cookies with egg white and sprinkle with cinnamon, almonds, and sugar. Bake for 10 minutes.

– MAKES 2 DOZEN COOKIES –

# *Vanilla Hearts*
## [Vanilje Hjerter]

Preheat oven to 350°. Beat butter and sugar until light and fluffy. Add egg, milk, and vanilla alternately with flour and baking powder. Knead dough and roll with a rolling pin to ½″ thick. Cut out hearts with cookie cutter. Arrange cookies on a greased cookie sheet and bake for 10 minutes. Hearts should be golden yellow.

– MAKES 2 DOZEN COOKIES –

10 TABLESPOONS BUTTER,
ROOM TEMPERATURE

½ CUP SUGAR

1 EGG

½ CUP MILK

1½ TEASPOONS VANILLA

2 CUPS FLOUR

1 TEASPOON BAKING POWDER

2 CUPS BLANCHED, GROUND ALMONDS

2 CUPS POWDERED SUGAR

1 EGG WHITE

1 TABLESPOON WATER OR COGNAC

FOOD COLORING (OPTIONAL)

# Marzipan Sweets

[Marsipan Konfekter]

*The marzipan adds a nice touch to any Christmas table. It keeps well for weeks if wrapped airtight, so I usually make an extra batch for my secret stash.*

The almonds must be very finely ground. Mix with powdered sugar and egg white. Add the water or cognac and work dough until easy to shape. Be careful not to overwork dough or it will become oily and gray. (Dough will be consistency of play dough.) Divide dough and shape into small balls, pigs, hearts, or any shape you choose. Add food coloring if desired. Garnish with melted chocolate, nuts, or candy sprinkles. Be creative!

– MAKES 30 CANDIES –

# Gingerbread House and Cookies

## [Pepper Kake Hus]

In a large bowl, beat shortening and sugar until creamy. Add all other ingredients, except 1 cup of flour. Stir and knead until dough is smooth. Wrap dough in an airtight wrap and refrigerate overnight.

Draw a design for the house you want to make and cut a pattern. Make the roof a little larger than the house to allow overlap.

Remove dough from refrigerator and preheat oven to 350°. Roll out half the dough using the reserved flour. Make sure baking table and rolling pin are well floured to prevent dough from sticking. Dough for the gingerbread house should be ½" thick. Arrange your pattern on the dough and cut around it. Don't cut out doors and windows before putting dough on a greased cookie sheet. This will prevent dough from

2 cups Shortening

2 cups Brown Sugar

2 tablespoons Cinnamon

2 tablespoons Ginger

2 teaspoons Cloves

¼ teaspoon Pepper

2 cups Dark Corn Syrup

4 Eggs

11 cups Flour

3 teaspoons Baking Soda

ICING

2 pounds Powdered Sugar

6 Egg Whites

1½ teaspoons Cream of Tartar

stretching. Bake gingerbread for about 10 minutes or until dough is light brown but without dark edges. Prepare icing while gingerbread bakes and cools.

ICING

Combine all ingredients and beat with an electric mixer for 10 minutes. (Icing will keep for several days in an airtight container.)

After gingerbread has cooled, arrange the house on a tray or lined cookie sheet. Fill a pastry bag with icing and use a medium-sized tip. Glue walls together using icing and let wall stay untouched for at least 30 minutes to allow icing to set. Add roof. You may have to hold it in place for awhile until it sets. Then, using more icing and candy, go wild decorating it. Make it a kid's dream come true.

*NOTE: This recipe is fool-proof: it does not crack or collapse. I have tried many different ways to make gingerbread houses, and have usually ended up with gingerbread shacks instead.*

Use remaining dough to make cookies. Roll dough a little thinner, cut, and bake for about 8 minutes.

# Roast Pork with Mushroom Sauce
[ S i n k e   S t e k ]

Preheat oven to 325°. Cut fat on top of roast into squares. Rub salt and pepper over entire roast. Place in roasting pan with 2 cups of water and cook for 2½ to 3 hours. You may need to add additional water as some of it evaporates.

## MUSHROOM SAUCE

Melt butter in a saucepan over low heat and add flour. Slowly add drippings while stirring. Add wine, soy sauce, bay leaf, and salt and pepper. In a separate pan, sauté mushrooms in a little butter, then add to sauce before serving.

– SERVES 8 –

5 POUNDS BONELESS PORK ROAST WITH FAT ON TOP

2 CUPS WATER

SALT AND PEPPER

MUSHROOM SAUCE

2 TABLESPOONS BUTTER

3 TABLESPOONS FLOUR

2½ CUPS ROAST DRIPPINGS

¼ CUP RED WINE

1 TEASPOON SOY SAUCE

¼ BAY LEAF

SALT AND PEPPER TO TASTE

1 POUND MUSHROOMS, CUT INTO SLIVERS

# Red Sour Cabbage

## [Rød Kål]

2 POUNDS RED CABBAGE

2 TEASPOONS SALT

2 TEASPOONS CARAWAY

2½ CUPS WATER

4 TABLESPOONS VINEGAR

4 TEASPOONS SUGAR

Cut cabbage into fine shreds and place with all other ingredients in a large pot. Bring to a boil. Cover pot, reduce heat, and simmer for 2½ hours. Add more water if necessary. Serve hot.

– SERVES 8 –

# Green Peas and Pearl Onions
[Grønne Erter og Små Løk]

Peel and clean onions. Sauté in butter for five minutes and add water to pan. Let cook slowly for 15 minutes, then add peas. Cook together for 5 minutes. Drain and serve with white, cooked bratwurst on the side. The bratwurst tastes much like traditional Norwegian Christmas sausage, Jule pølse.

– SERVES 8 –

¼ POUND PEARL ONIONS

1 TABLESPOON BUTTER

¼ CUP WATER

1 POUND PEAS

½ pound Ground Pork

½ pound Ground Beef

3 teaspoons Salt

1 Egg

4 tablespoons Corn Starch

1 teaspoon Pepper

½ teaspoon Cardamom

¼ teaspoon Ginger

2 cups Beef Stock or Water

Oil for frying

# Christmas Meat Patties

[Jule Kjøtt Kaker]

Mix all ingredients together and form into small patties. Fry over medium heat until brown on both sides and well done in the middle. These freeze very well.

– Makes 20 Patties –

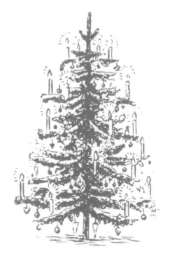

# Rice Cream with Berries
## [Ris Krem med Multebær]

*This delicious rice dish can be served any time of year but is a must on Christmas Eve. In Norway, we use cloud berries, or multebær, which look like yellowish orange raspberries but grow close to the ground in marshes high up in the mountains. People guard these berries with their lives. You will need to use strawberries or raspberries since cloud berries are not available in this country. Make extra rice pudding (p. 186) and save 6 cups for this dessert.*

Mix the cold rice pudding with the whipped cream, powdered sugar, and vanilla. Fold in strawberries (drain if frozen) and serve.

– SERVES 8 –

6 CUPS OF RICE PUDDING

1 PINT HEAVY CREAM, WHIPPED STIFF

2 CUPS POWDERED SUGAR

1 TEASPOON VANILLA

2 CUPS STRAWBERRIES